*With my deepest love,*

*I dedicate this book and the Image Keys within*

*to our beautiful PLANET EARTH...*

# INVITATION TO ENTER

You have before you a new kind of book,
a new energetic art form.
You are invited to fully interact and experience
its loving supportive energy.
As you turn to each new chapter,
it opens with the above image called "Crystal Waters".
After reading the title page of each chapter,
it is suggested that you place your left hand
over the words and image...
Close your eyes and feel the energy enter your Being.
Feel the connection forming between you, the image,
and the essence of the words
preparing you for the chapter ahead.
When you are ready, turn the page and begin.

# WELCOME

We are delighted to introduce
## Messages Of Universal Wisdom.
At the HEART of these messages are the Image Keys.

The Image Keys represent the colors and frequencies of
Creation and the Higher Dimensions.

They surround us with
UNCONDITIONAL LOVE, COMPASSION,
JOY, BEAUTY and BALANCE.

Choosing to focus upon these Higher Vibrations
draws these attributes into the
experiences and manifestations of our daily lives
and aids their expansion
into the collective consciousness that surrounds our planet.

The journey you take by entering these pages
is thus both very personal, and a contribution to
the ascension of Planet Earth and all who call her Home.

# THE CRYSTAL WHEEL

The Image before you is
THE CRYSTAL WHEEL.

The Crystal Wheel offers
a place of connection
to the HIGHER SELF and beyond.

As you read the introduction,
the energy of THE CRYSTAL WHEEL
is available to you.
assisting you with the
connection to your own Higher Self.

The CRYSTAL WHEEL also assists
your connection
to the essence of the words before you.

Messages Of Universal Wisdom  v

# THE PURPOSE

We are coming to the end of a
twenty-six thousand year grand cycle.

It is time for us to Evolve.

The Messages Of Universal Wisdom
held within this set of Image Keys
are a call to AWAKEN;
Awaken to the vastness of our being,
Awaken to our full and true potential,
Awaken to our life's purpose.

It is time for us to Evolve and to Create
a NEW WAY of Living
and Being within this World.

It is time to Create a New World built on
LOVE, PEACE and UNITY.

# THE IMAGE KEYS

The Image Keys unlock doorways
we are invited to walk through;
offering us connection to the vastness of our Being,
by providing stepping stones for our Transformation.

The Image Keys carry messages beyond the logic of words,
which speak to our heart and soul,
Awakening the Divine Blueprint held deep within our Being.

Working on all levels;
from within the cells of the physical body
to the very center of our Soul,
the Image Keys are here to
assist, support and sustain our growth and evolution.

Their healing energy reminds us
of our wholeness and inner perfection,
our connection to All That Is.

It is time to awaken and to remember who we truly are.

We are a part of the Divine Essence of the Universe.
We are loved beyond our greatest imaginings.
We each have an important role to play
in the evolution of Humanity on Earth.

# THE ALCHEMY

Within each Image Key, Crystals, Sacred Geometry,
Ascension Codes and the Universal Language of Light
create a unique interactive living energy
that is far greater than the sum of its parts.

As we choose to ALLOW the Image Keys
to integrate within our being,
we initiate the Alchemy within and around us,
refining the very substance from which we are made.

At every level synergy is experienced;
the Image Keys are Alchemy in action.

We are being called to accept this journey,
for ourselves, for Humanity and for the Earth.

It is a journey of Love and Divine Service to
ALL THAT IS.
Our participation is greatly needed.

# NEW ENERGIES

The Image Keys also capture and anchor
New Energies reaching the Earth due
to specific movements and alignments of the stars and planets.

These energies are playing a vital role
in the creation of our new reality.

The Integration of these New Energies into the
Fabric of our lives activates the Awareness of our True Self.

This integration is crucial to our evolution and survival.

The Image Keys facilitate and ease this integration.

The Image Keys invite all in their presence
to match their vibration.

The presence of the Image Keys throughout the world
has the potential to aid in the
Evolution of the Planet and the Whole of Humanity.

The crystal clear intention of the Image Keys
is to support the development of
a New Earth and a New Dream
for all people.

# Messages Of Universal Wisdom

## A Journey of Connection Through the Heart

### by
### Barbara Evans

*Spiritual Web Communications, LLC, Marlow, NH 03456*

Much of the information presented within *Messages Of Universal Wisdom* is intuitive in nature. It has not been scientifically tested. You are asked to use your own discernment as you read and to feel what is right for you.

Evolution in the sense used within the text refers to Spiritual Evolution and is not related to Darwinian Evolution.

The information presented is Spiritual in nature, without representing any Religion.

The intent and encouragement is to read, feel, experience and grow spiritually, not to replace medical or psychological consultation, diagnosis or treatment.

In all respects you are encouraged to follow the guidance within your own HEART. If you choose to use the intuitive information presented for your personal spiritual growth and the raising of your consciousness, the author and publisher assume no responsibility for your actions.

# Table of Contents

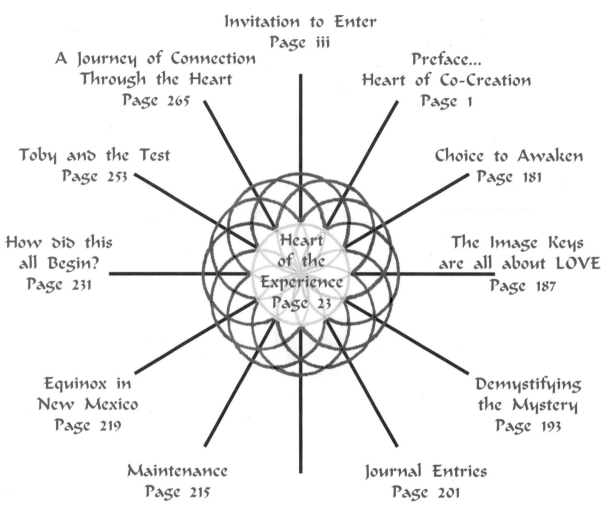

# Resources

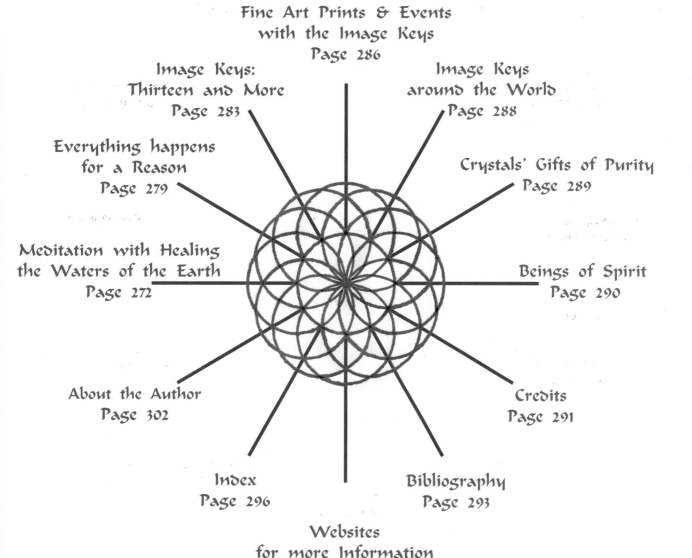

# Image Keys

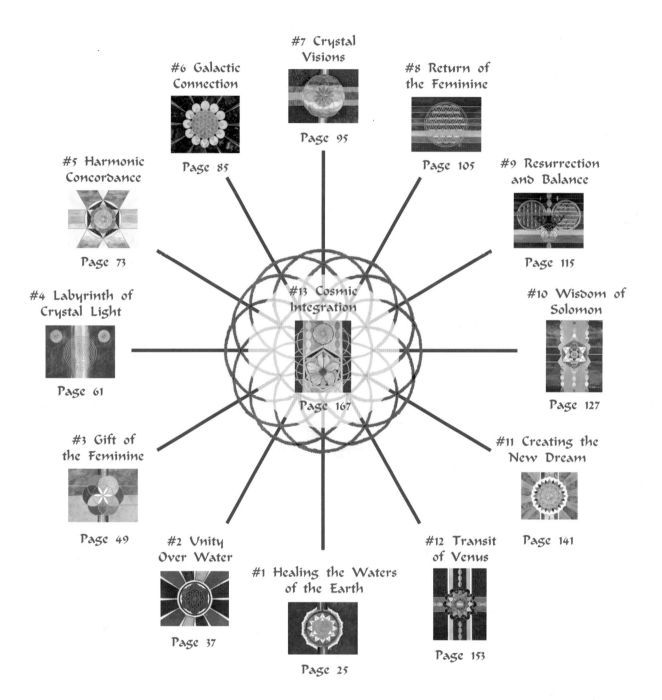

#7 Crystal Visions
Page 95

#6 Galactic Connection
Page 85

#8 Return of the Feminine
Page 105

#5 Harmonic Concordance
Page 73

#9 Resurrection and Balance
Page 115

#4 Labyrinth of Crystal Light
Page 61

#13 Cosmic Integration
Page 167

#10 Wisdom of Solomon
Page 127

#3 Gift of the Feminine
Page 49

#11 Creating the New Dream
Page 141

#2 Unity Over Water
Page 37

#1 Healing the Waters of the Earth
Page 25

#12 Transit of Venus
Page 153

To those I love...

...My Family: Nigel... Jon, Tim and Charlotte... Jean...

Friends, Teachers, Spirit Guides, and
many Authors who have inspired and
supported my Spiritual Awakening...

ArchAngel Metatron and Mary Magdalene,
Angels and ArchAngels,

Toby and Juno.

Without all of you by my side
this work would not have achieved physical form...

I am so grateful for the unique role
each of you has played and continues to play...

I thank you from the center of my HEART.

# PREFACE... HEART OF CO-CREATION

SETTING THE SCENE

MAJOR PLAYERS

UNLOCKING THE IMAGE KEYS

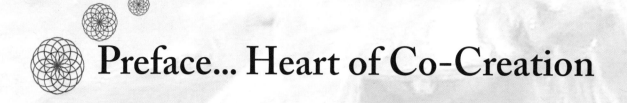

# Preface... Heart of Co-Creation

## Setting the scene...
## Introducing Major Players and Vital Concepts

The Image Keys are NEW to this world... They represent the colors, frequencies and patterns of Creation and the Higher Dimensions.

This is a book of FEELING and EXPERIENCING... The Image Keys interact with all levels of our being...

The descriptive words used within this, and other chapters provide a starting point. It is an introduction... offering one possible entry point into the vast, unlimited energy and form of each Image Key. You are encouraged to allow your own intuition to expand and guide you as you explore and connect with these patterns and frequencies on your own unique Soul journey.

For some who hold this book in their hands, no words will be necessary. They will open to each Image Key and begin a very personal interaction without assistance. For others the mind will require some understanding before allowing the HEART to begin the interaction.

The focus of the Preface is to introduce a few of the underlying concepts before we enter the core essence of the book. The core essence contains the Image Keys which are found within Chapter One, *Heart of the Experience.*

The intention of the Preface is to quiet the mind.

At this point I wish to make a request.... Please do not allow yourself to get stuck or stalled by any of the words... If there is something that you do not understand or do not wish to read... skim over it. Go straight to the Image Keys, if you like. The purpose of this book is to present the Image Keys... The words are only useful if they assist you personally to gain greater access to the beauty, joy and magnificence of the *Messages*

*Of Universal Wisdom* held within the Image Keys. These 13 Image Keys have the potential to interact with all levels of our being... Energy encoded within each Image Key offers to initiate a calibration of our energy fields to remind us of the powerful, spiritual beings we truly are. This is a book of FEELING and EXPERIENCING... of recognizing and acknowledging the HEART as the gateway to our TRUE INNER SELF.

# The Analogy of the Gourmet Cake

Each ingredient of the Image Keys can be compared to the ingredients of a cake. In both situations the selection of the ingredients and the skill with which they are combined determines the success and character of the finished product.

The basic ingredients of a cake are flour, eggs and sugar. Variations are possible, yet these ingredients form the basic structure, without which there would be no cake. Within the Image Keys, the Sacred Geometry takes on this basic, structural role.

Fruit, Nuts, Chocolate and Spices are among the great variety of extras that are chosen to give the cake its character. The Signature Crystals offer their individual gifts to influence the uniqueness of each Image Key.

Vanilla and Almond Essence give additional flavor. They are sometimes added, and sometimes not. These equate to the Flower Essences which are sometimes used with the Image Keys.

It is important for the cake to fully rise. To ensure this, baking powder is added... For the Image Keys, we allocate this role to the New Energies.

The Baker chooses and puts these ingredients together. The "magic" of the Baker is an important ingredient in itself. The Visionary Artist and Spirit Guides combine to take the role of Baker.

The cake batter is mixed and placed into an oven where the HEAT ENERGY transforms the batter into something new, something so much more than the individual ingredients. The Crystal Grid formed from the Alchemy Crystals is the "Oven" for the Image Keys. It is within the Crystal Grid that the energetic Environment is created to bring about the transformation from individual basic ingredients to the finished product... a new Image Key. There is one major difference. I place myself within this Energetic Oven created by the Crystal Grid.

To enjoy, appreciate and gain full nourishment from the cake does not require any understanding of the recipe or the cooking time involved... You will intuitively "know" whether you like it or not. Similarly with the Image Keys... it is the complete Image Key that is important to you. Knowing something of the ingredients and preparation is interesting, rather than essential. The nourishment and transformational energies presented within the completed Image Keys are for you to enjoy and to absorb into your body like energetic food.

As the receiver of this wonderful, large and rich cake, it is important that you use your own discernment... to eat only the portion size that is perfect for you in one sitting... to know when to stop, to rest and assimilate...and when to return another day for another piece. The same applies to the Image Keys... They are energetically active. How much is right for you on any particular day is entirely for you to determine.

Your job is to relax and enjoy the Image Keys, allowing them to nourish your Body, Mind and Soul.

My job as Visionary Artist is to collect, combine and facilitate the transformation of ingredients into the end product... then to present the Image Keys to nourish and enrich all levels of your Being.

# Awakening... Spiritual Growth... Transformation...

My own beliefs have changed dramatically since I consciously set foot upon this journey of Spiritual Awakening in August 1993. There has been a continual expansion in awareness of my place within the World and the Universe.

I know this process is still ongoing... I AM continuously growing, evolving and connecting more fully with my TRUE INNER SELF. My understanding of LIFE and my awareness of connections to ALL THAT IS are being refined and ever expanding.

I have become aware that I AM a Spiritual Being who has come into this physical body to experience and contribute to life on this planet at this particular moment of NOW. I have discovered that my closest spiritual companion is my Higher Self.

My Higher Self always has my best interests as a focus. Each person has their own unique Higher Self which has a far greater awareness and knowledge of the "big picture" than most humans experience. At this stage in human evolution the choice to become conscious of the relationship we have with our Higher Self is open to all.

For those who are searching for a new way forward in life, for a more harmonious, less stressful way of living within the world… the invitation, the challenge, and the excitement is to bring more of our Spiritual Higher Self into our physical body. In this way, we can live with more awareness and have greater access to the gifts and skills, wisdom and knowledge accrued in other lifetimes. Merging the Higher Self into our physical Body allows us to bring all of our gifts together NOW.

One purpose of the Image Keys is to assist this integration process with GRACE and EASE… to assist us to become ALL THAT WE ALREADY TRULY ARE.

As this integration takes place, we begin to feel more whole and complete. We begin to release our fears and feel touched by JOY in the center of our HEART. We begin to FEEL LIFE AT A WHOLE NEW LEVEL.

# Spiritual Hierarchy

Within the worlds beyond this world… in the higher dimensions… there are many Beings of Spirit whose focus is the expansion of LOVE and LIGHT, PEACE and COMPASSION… Some refer to these Beings of Spirit as the Spiritual Hierarchy.

The array of these Spiritual Beings is vast indeed… from Gods and Goddesses of all cultures who have lived upon the Earth to Angels and ArchAngels and so many more such as Ascended Masters like Jesus, Buddha and St. Germain.

# Connections to the Beings of Spirit

The possibility of connecting and communicating directly with these Beings of Spirit on a personal level is increasing as we each, as individuals, open up and clear our energy fields and raise our energetic vibrations.

My first connection was to my father who visited me in a dream two months after his passing from this world. This first contact was followed several years later by a connection to White Eagle, a Native American Guide, and then Merlyn of the Authurian Legends.

Now as I continue to clear my energy fields, I feel a direct connection to a wide range of these Spiritual Beings of LOVE and LIGHT... Light Beings, who assist the evolution of Humanity upon the Earth.

# Signature Guides of the Image Keys

The Signature Guides of the Image Keys are members of the Spiritual Hierarchy. I have been aware of their involvement since the Co-Creation of the very first Image Key. The Spirit Being or Beings who are to guide the creative process step forward as preparations begin. They direct the sacred geometry structure to be used and the choice of crystals to be incorporated. The Signature Guides also add their own spiritual healing vibrations and frequencies to the fabric, essence and alchemy of the piece.

I use the word fabric to mean the intricate, synergistic combination of physical watercolor paper, paint and energies that are so much more than the individual components. The fabric is the energy matrix which creates the essence or the spiritual nature of the Image Key... its unique, personal signature.

I often refer to a Guide "over-lighting" an Image Key or my work in general... To over-light is to guide and watch over, to ensure that the project stays on track. I now recognize ArchAngel Metatron as the Spiritual Guide who is in charge of this project. He over-lights the entire process.

# Image Keys

The Image Keys are a series of Paintings that I began in September 2003... This book holds 13 Image Keys within the core chapter, *Heart of the Experience.*

The details of design for each Image Key are received from my Spirit Guides, together with the Affirmations, Poems and Decrees. I don't physically see the members of the Spiritual Hierarchy that I work with, nor do I hear their voices... The name of the Guide simply floats into my mind. From the subtle way I feel, I know that they are with me. This happens constantly when I am painting.

The Spirit Guides provide their information in pieces through inspiration and instructions coming through me. The pieces are given over a period of days, weeks or even longer. It is then my job to work out how to put the "puzzle pieces" together. Sometimes, sudden changes are made as I am drawing the Image Key... When this happens, it is instantaneous, without any conscious thought on my part, always refining the earlier plan.

## Co-Creation and Channeling

The Image Keys are a Co-Creation in that many BEINGS contribute to their formation. I, as a Visionary Artist within a physical body, have the job of collecting all of the pieces... Many of these pieces are energetic and not visible to the human eye... Once collected within my Being, I weave together the different energetic strands and translate them into physical form, visible and tangible within this physical world. In this way, others have the opportunity to work with the same combinations of energy.

Certain aspects within the Image Keys are directly channeled. Although a part of the overall Co-Creation, I see these aspects as additional blessings upon the work.

During a channeling, the energy flows through me while I effectively stand back and allow it to happen without interfering or affecting the energy... This allows the PURITY of the message to be maintained. This happens at certain times, both when writing and painting. The gift of information received during channeling is its PURITY. This is a top priority as I work... It is always within my conscious awareness to maintain the PURITY.

Co-Creation requires greater action on my part... I am very much a member of the team... the member that just happens to be in a physcial body. I have an active role to play in the creation of the Image Keys. The guides make me think. They give me puzzles and clues that I need to work out before the pieces are put together... before I am able to hold and translate the information into its final form. As this happens, it ensures my own evolution and awakening... I cannot move forward with the work until I *get* it myself.

The work before you represents my very personal journey... I have lived every aspect of these Image Keys... I am writing about my life experience. Through the intensity of this experience, the work is presented to help others… Those who choose to read and actively participate in this book… may, through their own unique and special journey, discover deeper levels of themselves. This is what I have been doing… discovering myself and the reason I am here walking the Earth at this particular time. As this takes place on an individual level, it contributes to raising the consciousness of Humanity and thus assists the Earth in her ascension process.

# Language of Light

The Angels speak through the Language of Light… We on Earth may receive this in the form of color, "squiggle writing", or as sound. All three of these forms are involved with the Image Keys.

It is this language of the Angels that the Image Keys hold.

The messages within the Image Keys offer an opportunity… They offer to assist us to connect with the wholeness and fullness of our TRUE SELF. We are being invited to allow the *Messages Of Universal Wisdom,* presented through the Language of Light, Sacred Geometry, Crystal Energies and the Blessings of the Spirit Beings to be absorbed by all levels of our Being… physical, emotional, mental and spiritual. As this happens… the process leads to a raising of our Consciousness… a raising of our Spiritual Awareness. As our Consciousness rises in its energy vibrations, all other aspects of our Being are brought into alignment.

As you introduce the Image Keys into your life, it is important to follow your own intuition. Allow your intuition to strengthen within. Know that the level of interaction between you and the Image Keys will be affected by your intent… the Prayer within your HEART. This is a journey of SELF-EMPOWERMENT.

We are embarking on a journey of Awakening and Remembering, connecting with the vastness of our Being… finding our full and true potential… becoming ONE with the magnificence of who we truly are.

# Sacred Geometry

Sacred Geometry can be described as the Language of the Universe… Its patterns, relationships and harmonics are found throughout creation. Sacred Geometry is fundamental to the composition of the Image Keys providing the structural patterns upon which the other energies are woven.

My approach to Sacred Geometry is as an intuitive artist and builder. I work through the essence of the geometry, rather than the mathematics. It is through this essence that my relationship with geometry has developed and the Image Keys have been Co-Created.

The geometry to which all the Image Keys are linked is The Flower of Life. The Flower of Life is both simple and complex... Within its form are held many secrets. This very ancient and sacred symbol is found in sacred sites throughout the world.

The function of the Sacred Geometry within each Image Key is beyond the words of our human language. This geometry functions in fullness without the need for verbal description.

However, early on in my work with the Flower of Life, my attention was drawn to the fact that there is a male and female form... I was both fascinated and captivated as this aspect became a vital theme within the Image Keys. I therefore chose to introduce the Sacred Geometry of the Image Keys through the Masculine and Feminine Energies... This is just one aspect... There is so much more.

*Masculine Flower of Life*
The central column of Petals runs vertically through the Geometry.

*Feminine Flower of Life*
The central row of Petals runs horizontally throughout the Geometry.

Within the Flower of Life, the Vesica Piscis and Genesis Pattern are both found.

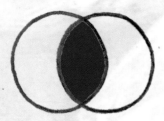

**Vesica Piscis**
Vertical "Almond" Shape

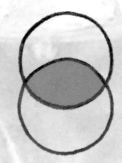

**Vesica Piscis**
Horizontal "Eye" Shape

A Vesica Piscis is formed by interlocking two circles through the central point of each. The central almond shape, or if rotated, the eye is known as the Vesica. The Vesica represents creation and is considered to be one of the most sacred shapes.

**Male Genesis Pattern**
The two central Petals are vertical.

The Genesis Pattern is composed of seven circles. The alignment of the "petals" within the central circle is an identifying factor in the "gender" of the geometry.

Within the Male Genesis Pattern, the two central inner petals... shown in blue... are vertical, following the line of the blue petals in the Male Flower of Life in the previous illustration.

Within the Female Genesis Pattern, the two central inner petals... shown in deep pink... are horizontal, following the form within the Female Flower of Life of the previous illustration. The second pair of paler pink petals show a "V" shape, which is often used symbolically to represent the female form, the vessel or womb.

**Female Genesis Pattern**
The two central Petals are horizontal; the two upper petals form a "V", a symbol of the female form.

The Unity Symbol is formed by placing the Male and Female Genesis Patterns together. The Unity Symbol represents Unity, Peace, Wholeness and the ending of the age of duality. As the Male and Female Genesis Patterns intertwine, twelve petals naturally form a Lotus Flower at the HEART of the Unity Symbol in the center of the geometry.

*Unity Symbol*
with combined
Male and Female Lotus Petals

This symbol is present within the Image Keys from the very beginning of *Messages Of Universal Wisdom*. Beautiful, in its simplicity, the Unity Symbol is the most important symbol within the Image Keys.

As with major notes within a symphony... these geometries are played over and over in varying combinations to initiate the Balance of Divine Energies. Balance is achieved through the sacred union of Divine Masculine with Divine Feminine to create Wholeness and Unity... the androgynous innocence of the Divine Child.

## Signature Crystals

The Signature Crystals are equally fundamental within the Image Keys, contributing significantly to the Intent of each piece. They often include new crystals that I am guided to bring into my collection as part of the preparation for each new Image Key. New crystals bring additional and very specific energies into the series. The energies of the Signature Crystals are actively channeled into the fabric of the Image Key.

*Ajoite Crystal*
Signature Crystal for *"Healing the Waters of the Earth"*

This rare Ajoite Crystal is one of the first to be used as a Signature Crystal... within the Image Key #1, *Healing the Waters of the Earth*... Its energy was channeled into the turquoise paint surrounding the white twelve-pointed star.

# Alchemy Crystals

The Alchemy Crystals are the great array of crystals involved with an individual Image Key. They contribute to the overall alchemy in a synergistic way, rather than standing out as individuals. The Alchemy Crystals come from many countries around the world: India, Peru, South Africa, Indonesia, the United States, Siberia, Morocco, the Czech Republic and others. They bring the energies of the land in which they were formed. This subtly contributes to the overall essence… connecting the Image Keys to all the continents of the Earth.

Alchemy Crystals are used within the Crystal Grid set up for the Creation of each individual Image Key.

# Crystal Grid

A Crystal Grid is a layout of crystals. A new Crystal Grid is laid out on the floor of my studio for the Creation of each Image Key.

*The Magdalene Grid set up in the Studio*
Crystals surround the work area

This Crystal Grid completely surrounds me while I work. There is a specific geometrical pattern to the grid… It mirrors the main geometry of the Image Keys… the Genesis Pattern and Unity Symbol.

The Crystal Grid has the effect of building a Sacred Space of crystal energy around me while I am working… This supports my energy and enhances my connections to my Higher Self, my I AM Presence and the Spirit Guides. At the same time, the Crystal Grid protects the space and the energy connections which contribute to the overall energy of the finished painting… the new Image Key.

As the series of Image Keys has progressed, larger crystals have been used and the area of the Crystal Grid has expanded within my studio.

# New Energies

The New Energies are discussed throughout this book. These are new frequencies that are bombarding the entire planet at this time in our history. They come from the particular way that the planets and stars are aligned. The alignments are followed and predicted by Astrologers. Information concerning their significance is being channeled by several very sensitive and gifted people who have refined their ability to receive messages from beyond the veil. One of my favorite messengers is Celia Fenn, located in South Africa. Celia channels ArchAngel Michael and posts monthly messages on her website. Celia's messages touch my heart and have been a vital part of my journey with the Image Keys. These and similar messages offer us an opportunity to begin to comprehend at least some aspects of the Divine Plan for the evolution of Mother Earth and all of her inhabitants.

These New Energies are triggering energetic shifts which have been predicted by many of the major ancient civilizations throughout time. These energies are causing us to raise our energetic, vibrational frequency, to become physically less dense, and to be filled with more Light, Love and Joy.

As with all change, we have a choice in how we are going to approach it. We can flow with the changes, adapting and growing as we go along; or, we can resist and fight against them. The New Energies will keep coming… Their arrival is *not* part of our personal choice. Our personal choice was to incarnate and to be here NOW to experience this Change of Life on Earth, whether we are currently sensitive to it, or not.

One of the major purposes of the Image Keys is to EASE OUR WAY. They can assist us to flow with the New Energies coming in. They can assist with the integration of these New Energies into the Heart of our Being and into the Heart of Mother Earth, so that we may make these shifts with the maximum amount of Grace and Ease possible... We are in the process of birthing a New Age of LOVE and PEACE...

# Alchemy

The Image Keys are truly about Alchemy.

Alchemy is the refining of our constituent parts. It is the refining of all levels of our Being, to reveal the TRUTH, BEAUTY and JOY of who we truly are, revealing the UNCONDITIONAL LOVE, COMPASSION and PERFECTION within us.

You may be drawn to return to an Image Key many times, or perhaps, many of them many times. Each time you are likely to be in a different place. There is potential for the interaction between you and the Image Key to evolve. As you grow and change, what the Image Key has to offer grows and changes, too. This is because there are so many levels built into each Image Key during its creation. As you evolve you are able to access new levels within the Image Key. How conscious you are of this process will vary from person to person and from moment to moment.

You are invited to accept the Image Keys as Spiritual Energy Companions for LIFE as you grow in consciousness and spiritual awareness.

# Complements

Each Image Key is accompanied by an Affirmation, Poem, Decree and Story. The Affirmations and Poems were channeled from my Spirit Guides early on during this process... after the completion of the thirteenth Image Key, yet before the book had begun to take shape... with the Decrees coming much later in the process.

Each of the Image Key stories is similar, yet unique. I introduce you to the circumstances and inspirations behind the particular Image Key together with its Sacred Geometry, Signature Guides and Signature Crystals. The intention of providing this information within the story is to offer points of reference... which can offer a WAY IN. The story in each case is a simple introduction as the vastness and unlimited potential of each Image Key is beyond words. As you read, I encourage you to be open and to allow your own intuition to guide you.

At a relatively late stage during the editing of the book, ArchAngel Metatron and Mary Magdalene stepped forward to provide some very special messages about the individual Image Keys. You will find these messages following the story of each Image Key within *Heart of the Experience*.

# Core Information

The Image Keys within *Heart of the Experience* are the Core Information being presented.

A Key is used to unlock something which is locked. The information held within the Image Keys has the potential to unlock the Divine Blueprint of perfection which we each carry deep inside ourselves. The unlocking takes place in stages allowing a slow release in manageable steps.

In this way the Image Keys are suitable for all who are inspired to use them. It is a process of awakening to the fullness of Who We Are through the raising of our Consciousness...

As this happens, we become more aware of how connected we all are... to each other and to every living organism on the planet... We begin to recognize the ONENESS.

We initiate the process of remembering simply by changing our mind about where we place our focus. It is a choice. We can choose LOVE, LIGHT, JOY, BALANCE and ABUNDANCE for ALL. As we constantly choose to focus on positive energies and positive attributes, our frequencies and vibrations begin to rise.

The Image Keys and their *Messages Of Universal Wisdom* are here to assist in this process... They embody LOVE, LIGHT, JOY and many other positive attributes... The Image Keys hold and anchor these higher vibrations. As we each choose to change and release our old patterns, the Image Keys invite us to match their higher vibrations. In this way the Image Keys offer us a focal point of Higher Consciousness.

# Unlocking the Image Keys

By the end of 2004, the series had grown to 13 Image Keys... My understanding of their significance was just beginning to expand. The next step was to learn how to access the information which they hold. I needed to understand how to place the Key into the Lock so that it can begin to most effectively do its job.

As I began working with each Image Key, it rapidly became apparent that there are many ways to initiate this interactive process.

You may simply focus upon the Image Key of your choice, becoming aware of the different aspects within that are calling to you. Take your time... notice and acknowledge any feelings that arise within you. Notice and acknowledge any memories that suddenly and unexpectedly flow into your mind.

You may choose to have the Image Key radiating its energy into the space around you by having the book open with an Image Key displayed so that you can focus upon it easily during your day. You may wish to have it nearby as you sleep at night.

Trust that the energies are working around you whether you feel them or not.

Each Image Key may also be used as a focal point for meditation, either with your eyes open, gently focusing upon the image, or with the Image Key placed in front of you with your eyes closed. The energy interaction between you and the Image Key will occur whether your eyes are open or closed.

As you sit in silent meditation, I suggest holding the Intent within your mind for the energies of the Image Key to interact with your energy fields through all levels of your Being. If meditation is not something you normally do, you can replace this word with contemplation. Sit and contemplate the Image Key, either with your eyes open or closed. How long you choose to sit in this focused way is for you to feel... Allow yourself to feel, to experience, to be intuitively guided by your Higher Self and Spirit Guides.

Sometimes you may find you feel as though you are being drawn into the Image Key... or that the geometric patterns begin to move... or that they no longer lie flat on the page… or you may not experience any of these… or you may experience something I have not mentioned… All are completely appropriate.

Your interaction with the Image Keys is an opportunity to empower your own intuition.

# Unlocking the Image Keys by Sound

The next step is to bring in the action of the VOICE by reading the Affirmation out loud. Our voices are powerful sound tools. To speak the words of the Affirmation will take the interaction to a new level. If you are not used to doing this, it may seem strange at first… Relax and allow the words to flow. As your voice sounds the words, focus your eyes upon the Image Key.

Realizing the POWER of the words we choose to speak and the unique sounds within our voice is another step in Awakening. It is also making a definite statement to the Universe that you are willingly taking an active part. You are not just reading for information as an observer… You are participating with the intention of bringing about positive changes within your life.

The greater your focus, feeling and intent as you sound the powerful Affirmation, the greater the connection you will make. It is suggested that if you wish to *set* this energy to keep it working within you… repeat the Affirmation three times.

The Poem takes you deeper still into the essence of the Image Key. Again, repeat the words aloud, speaking them with focused Intent, by which I mean, really "feeling" the words as they are spoken.

The Decree naturally follows the earlier steps. Each Decree begins with the words I AM.

From my own understanding, the use of the words "I AM" calls upon the Divine Spark within you to become active and involved in your life. Your Divine Spark is part of your I AM Presence. Calling upon your I AM Presence is calling upon the highest, most divine part of your Being…

Use the Decree when you are ready, willing and prepared for what is pronounced within the Decree to BE your reality.

# How the Image Keys Work

The Image Keys work through our energetic fields, and particularly through the emotional system, to support the release of energy blockages and to encourage the integration of the energy codes and the language of light that form the *Messages Of Universal Wisdom*. They have the potential to activate and calibrate all levels of our Being.

An energy blockage within the emotional system occurs when we experience a powerful *negative experience*. To get over it, we stuff it inside and pretend it never happened. In this way, we can get on with our life quickly, rather than taking the time to be loving and compassionate with ourselves. Love and compassion is required to release the emotional trauma from our systems. These emotional blockages have happened to all of us as we have grown up within this world. Some people are more sensitive than others; some are more prone to "stuffing" than others.

*Barbara's Aura, photo taken in 2000*
Reds, magenta and violet can be seen together with 5 mini moving orbs.

When we collect enough of these emotional blockages over time, or they are dense enough, they begin to affect our physical structure... We begin to develop *dis-ease* within our tissues and cells... This is one of the reasons our physcial bodies show signs of aging.

The energetic emotional body inter-penetrates the physical body following the exact design down to levels within each individual cell, then extending out beyond the surface of the physical body. This contributes to the creation of our Aura. The Aura is the energy that some people can see and feel that surounds each one of us.

As a blockage is released, some of that emotion is often felt again... If this occurs while working with the Image Keys, it is important to know and understand that it is happening at this time so that it can be released... You do not need to relive the event... just acknowledge it, and allow it to pass. It is important to be gentle and loving with yourself, to take plenty of rest and drink plenty of water as you are doing energetic healing... Emotions are surfacing to be released, to lighten your burden. As blockages are released, interaction with the Image Keys deepen and we become more open to receive their messages... offering us greater opportunities to initiate the Divine Blueprint already held within our Being.

Now it is time to venture forth and meet the Thirteen Image Keys...

Time to ALLOW their energies to

IGNITE our PASSION,

FIRE our UNCONDITIONAL LOVE,

and INSPIRE COMPASSION...

both within our SELF

and within our LIFE.

# HEART OF THE EXPERIENCE

THIRTEEN IMAGE KEYS REVEALED

AFFIRMATIONS ● POEMS ● DECREES

TWELVE SURROUND THE ONE

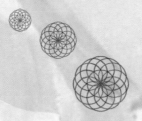

# #1 Healing the Waters of the Earth

*ONE… New Beginnings…*

ONE is about the individual…
the individual is a hologram for the WHOLE.

*Healing the Waters of the Earth* encourages the opening and healing of the HEART. This heart opening provides a foundation for the wholeness of the individual to manifest. Through the individual HEART opening, the opportunity of new beginnings for the Whole is offered… the Whole Planet… the Whole Universe.

We are ALL ONE.

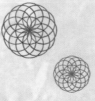

# *Healing the Waters of the Earth*
## *Image Key #1*

Affirmation #1

I ALLOW the vibration of Love to open and heal my heart.

# *Healing the Waters of the Earth*

## Poem #1

The energy speaks to MY HEART,

Connecting through to MY SOUL,

Gently healing emotional wounds,

Encouraging my heart to open...

Allowing the journey to begin.

## Decree #1

**I AM the Embodiment of LOVE.**

# Healing the Waters of the Earth
## Image Key #1

## I AM the Embodiment of LOVE.

The birth of *Healing the Waters of the Earth* resulted from many diverse pieces of my life coming together... a circle completed... This journey had taken me thirty years. Suddenly things were making sense at a new level never before contemplated... I went from being a biologist to an energy worker to a visionary artist, each and every step vital to the creation of the whole.

The trigger for this new level of being was my presence at a conference entitled "The Water of LIFE" held in September 2003 at the Omega Institute in New York State. Biologists, ecologists, water engineers and spiritual teachers of varying backgrounds filled the Conference Hall. The language of the scientists was very familiar, yet I knew within my heart that I was present as a *healing artist*.

My heart called for a powerful response, urging me to do my part for the Waters of our planet. During the drive home, I made a spiritual commitment to myself, my guides and the Divine Creator to bring all of my gifts together... to create a painting for "healing the waters of the Earth". The crucial intent was to create a painting that is energetically active and can contribute to the healing, evolution and ascension of our planet Earth in a very real sense... not just a pretty picture to place upon the wall.

The fulfillment of this mission began almost immediately. I drew upon all I had learned in this lifetime together with intuitive remembering from other lifetimes. I carefully prepared sacred space for the creation of this special painting. Then I called upon all of the Spiritual Beings who are working through LOVE and LIGHT for the benefit of all on Earth. Particularly I called upon those Spirit Beings who work lovingly with the Waters... oceans, lakes, rivers, streams, waterfalls and raindrops. I asked these guides to show themselves within the painting if this was something they chose to do.

The painting took a week to complete... It was the most intense work I had ever done up to that point... working... channeling... writing... being guided in every step from early morning until evening.

At this stage I had no idea this would be the first in a series of paintings that would become known as the Image Keys.

It became clear during the creative process that the energy of the painting was active on many levels… Yes, it has the ability to contribute to the healing of the Waters on a planetary level… It also has the ability to work with the Waters within a single Human body and everywhere in between depending upon the intention of the user.

*Crystal Waters*
prototype for "*Healing the Waters of the Earth*"

The prototype for this painting had been created just a few weeks earlier. The prototype was called *Crystal Waters*. It had been within my portfolio throughout the Omega Conference. Now the geometry of *Crystal Waters* was to be expanded in order to facilitate the full connection to the planet and the Water Element. This new geometric painting became the first Image Key.

The following series of "fade geometries" highlight some of the major parts of each Image Key. They take you on a journey into the sacred geometry itself… offering you the opportunity to deepen your connection to the *Messages Of Universal Wisdom* held within.

A golden Unity Symbol with silver "lotus" petals is at the center of Image Key #1, *Healing the Waters of the Earth*. The intense pink carries the energy of Rose Quartz, a crystal connected with the heart. This Unity Symbol brings balance to Masculine and Feminine energies… offering purity of connection to the creative forces.

*Unity Symbol*

*Icosahedron*

The Unity Symbol nestles within a silver Icosahedron... This three dimensional geometry has twenty sides. Each side is an equilateral triangle. In a cross section it appears as a hexagon. The Icosahedron has been associated with the Water Element since the time of the Greek philosopher, Plato.

Moving outwards, the white twelve-pointed star reflects the geometry of the Unity Symbol... Similar points are connected with straight lines instead of circles... This star also assists with the balancing of Masculine and Feminine Energies. The turquoise color surrounding the white star carries the energy of Ajoite, Chrysocolla and Larimar, all powerful Water Element Crystals.

*Twelve-Pointed Star*

The Amethyst/purple circle offers the energy of Divine Connection. It is surrounded by twelve emerald green petals ... Traditionally twelve such petals are used to represent the Heart Chakra within Eastern Spiritual Teachings. An aura of yellow sunlight surrounds the entire central geometry, bathing us in the light of the Divine.

*Amethyst, Emerald & Aura of Yellow Sunlight*

The rainbows signify connection to the HEART of the UNIVERSE above and the HEART of the EARTH below. As the rainbow light travels through the central geometry, it interacts with the life force encompassed within and is itself transformed...

The rainbow light transmitted to the Earth thus reflects this change through the reversal in the rainbow colors.

*Rainbows*

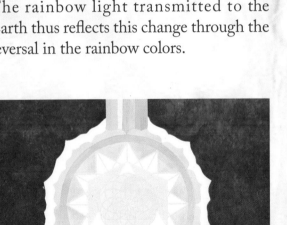

*Blue Background*

The deep blue background is filled with the energy of insight and self knowledge... characteristics contributed by the crystals, Azurite and Lapis Lazuli. The Blue reminds us of all Waters... oceans, lakes, rivers, streams, rainfall and the water within living organisms... plants, animals, microorganisms and HUMANS.

Each crystal within the photograph has an energetic connection to the Water Element. Their energies enhance the geometry. Pink, green and turquoise crystals particularly affect the HEART and EMOTIONAL SYSTEM. They offer nurturing, release, healing, inner peace and LOVE, both to human systems and to the Planet as a whole.

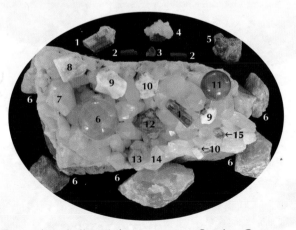

*Water Element Crystals*

1-Green Tourmaline, 2-Epidote, 3-Clear Apóphyllite, 4-Green Apophyllite, 5-Aquamarine on Smokey Quartz, 6-Rose Quartz, 7-Quartz Cluster, 8-Aquamarine, 9-Ajoite, 10-Larimar, 11-Aventurine, 12-Chrysocolla, 13-Amazonite, 14-Kunzite, and 15-Dioptase.

The colors within the painting are selected to represent the crystals… The use of color throughout the Image Keys is determined by the crystal energies being incorporated into them.

*Healing the Waters of the Earth* and the other Image Keys work on many levels… You may imagine yourself within the central geometry receiving this healing transformative energy. Within your mind, you may also place our planet Earth within the geometry and imagine the entire world receiving these *Messages Of Universal Wisdom*.

The life changing point for me during this intense week was the painting of the background blue… In one particular area the paint appeared not to *stick*. As I looked more closely, I realized there was a face… Instantaneously and instinctively I knew this was Poseidon, Greek God of the SEA… This was not someone I thought of frequently… It has been over twenty years since I visited Greece, and even longer since I read any Greek Mythology… Poseidon came OUT OF THE BLUE… He answered my call and showed himself within the painting.

*Poseidon outlined*

*Can you find Poseidon in the background?*

As I searched the rest of the background I found others too, including Coventina, British Goddess of Water and Mary, Mother of Jesus.

Since that day many people have searched the patterns and swirls within this deep blue background… Many see what I see… Others find other Beings and Creatures who have blessed this piece and shown their presence.

The appearance of Poseidon was a mighty confirmation that my prayers had been heard and acted upon… I had done what I had set out to do. The Image Key was being guided and supported by the members of the Spiritual Hierarchy.

My life was changed forever.

Coventina can be found centered within this area of the background blue. I see a beautiful and graceful face with the eyes looking down. She is not as easy to find as Poseidon... and there are other beings within the same area which complicate the situation and can draw your attention away from Coventina. As you focus on the swirls and patterns, can you find Coventina? Do you see any other Beings? Do you feel their presence? Do any names float into your mind?

*Coventina*

*Healing the Waters of the Earth* is a very special Image Key because it represents the beginning. It is filled with LOVE and COMPASSION and offers to share these gifts with all who choose to respond. It is the foundation piece. It is the door opener.

# ArchAngel Metatron
## speaks* for Healing the Waters of the Earth:

I AM
the door opener,
the foundation piece.

I can help you to take the first steps
on this new and exciting journey to find yourself;
the SELF that is already present and magnificent,
yet deeply hidden within your being.

My greatest joy is the flow of Life Force, the fluidity of LOVE.
To see you bathe in this beauty
and feel the touch of the Angels upon your skin and within your heart.

My job is to initiate this process of awakening
within your HEART and MIND.

I invite you to participate.

These Image Keys are a gift to Humanity
from the Spiritual Hierarchy,
to EASE your way,
to accelerate your awakening
in a graceful, delicate, sensitive fashion.

They present to you delights and energies
of the Higher Dimensions in visible physical form.
They are for you to enjoy and embody.

*as channelled by Barbara Evans

# Mary Magdalene
## speaks* for Healing the Waters of the Earth:

Water in its pristine, energetically vital form
carries the energies of the Divine Feminine.

This energy is flowing, nurturing, and life giving
to all who inhabit this planet Earth.

Healing the Waters of the Earth
connects with the Divine Feminine aspects
of Water within the Earth
and within your body
recalibrating the energies within
to once more sing the song
of the Divine Feminine in FORM.

May tears of LOVE and COMPASSION
cleanse your HEART and SOUL.

*as channelled by Barbara Evans

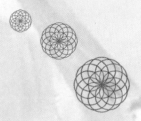

# #2 Unity Over Water

*TWO… Polarity and Balance…*

TWO… represents the coming together of opposites,
the poles of duality… to create Balance and Unity.

*Unity Over Water* assists us to achieve Balance and Unity
within all aspects of our lives. The central geometry in *Unity
Over Water* is the Unity Symbol placed over the Flower of
Life. With the gift of Unity, the skills of Balance act as a Key
to unlock the knowledge and wisdom of the Universe.

Within the individual this becomes an awakening
and a connection to one's Inner Knowing.

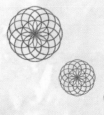

# Unity Over Water
## Image Key #2

## Affirmation #2

I ALLOW the rainbow rays to activate my Inner Knowing.

# *Unity Over Water*

Poem #2

Rainbow rays...

Drawn into the center of my being,

Providing strength and healing,

Unlock and activate knowledge held deep within.

Decree #2

**I AM fully connected to my Inner Knowing.**

# Unity Over Water
## Image Key #2

## I AM fully connected to my Inner Knowing.

**U**nity Over Water followed rapidly after *Healing the Waters of the Earth*. I was excited and inspired by the energy flowing through me in a way that could not be ignored… I had to paint!

Already the importance of the Unity Symbol was establishing itself within the Image Keys. The guidance was to place the Unity Symbol over the center of the Flower of Life. The Flower of Life symbol has been discovered in many ancient sacred sites around the world. The symbol was recorded in those ancient times… like clues for us to find and interpret as we enter the Age of Aquarius. According to Drunvalo Melchizedek in *The Ancient Secret of the Flower of Life*, these world-wide sites include Ireland, England, Greece, Turkey, Israel, Egypt, China, and Tibet.

The Genesis Pattern forming the basis of the Unity Symbol can be extracted from the Flower of Life. These two geometries are deeply and inextricably connected.

*Genesis Pattern*

*Genesis Pattern within the Flower of Life*

As the painting took shape the feeling grew within me... The Unity Symbol within this Image Key can be compared to a combination lock in the center of a safe door... where, upon turning the lock, the door opens and the contents can be accessed.

*Unity Symbol*

*Flower of Life*

The Unity Symbol is placed over the center of the Flower of Life unlocking the information held within. *Unity Over Water* assists us to access the mysteries of the Universe to which we belong. The vibrations of Amethyst found within the double circle support and protect this inner geometry. A double circle traditionally surrounds the Flower of Life.

For a symbol to hold information is one thing... for us to be able to access and integrate this knowledge into our physical awareness is quite a different matter. The golden yellow light is a celebration bursting forth before us... unlocking, accessing and confirming the importance of this Image Key to the development of our Inner Knowing.

*Sunburst*

*Rainbow Colors*

The colors of the rainbow, also relating to the colors of the seven major energy centers of the human body, radiate out from the central geometry. As I worked on these colors and crystals, the presence of Merlyn and King Arthur were clearly and strongly felt. This piece connects to Ancient Britain, Merlyn, King Arthur and Stonehenge. Merlyn and King Arthur are Spirit Beings who work tirelessly for the evolution of Life and PEACE on Earth.

It is a powerful Image Key. There is something very masculine about its energy... The Flower of Life is presented in the masculine form, but it is more than that... It is the part played by these two guides, Merlyn and King Arthur, who represent the "right use" of Masculine power and energy.

*Azurite on Quartz Cluster*
encourages insight.

*Lapis Lazuli on Quartz Cluster*
encourages self knowledge.

The vibrations of Azurite and Lapis Lazuli found within the background blue of *Healing the Waters of the Earth* are now found within the blues of the central geometry of *Unity Over Water*. Lapis Lazuli and Azurite are both Wind Element stones and support our connection to the Spiritual World.

This Image Key represents a quest... a quest to find our wholeness, our Divine Perfection in physical form. *Unity Over Water* will then assist us to use the awakened Divine Perfection wisely both for ourselves and in service to others.

***Azurite***
within the blue of the Flower of Life.

This Image Key is perfect for when strength is needed... whether this is an increase in physical, mental, emotional or spiritual strength. Call upon Merlyn and King Arthur to assist you to find the strength that you need in order to fulfill your life's mission on Earth... to BE all you planned to BE before beginning this incarnation.

***Lapis Lazuli***
within the blue of the Unity Symbol,
the underlying Flower of Life is also clearly visible.

*Unity Over Water* is an Image Key that encourages you to become aware of your own Inner Knowing... It assists you to consciously connect with your Higher Self. It brings the guidance and wisdom of your Higher Self into this physical body. As this occurs, you may find that you begin to recognize and trust your own inner knowing to new and deeper levels.

*Unity Over Water* also encourages the "right use" and respect for our Earth's waters. It assists the waters of our planet to regain their crystalline structure, their inner strength, by initiating the remembrance of the Divine Blueprint.

Pristine waters, as found in active Sacred Springs around the world, have a natural crystalline structure. This crystalline structure reflects the nature of water as it once existed everywhere.

I did not choose the name of this Image Key. Like all the others, it was channeled from the Spiritual Hierarchy. *Unity Over Water* is a strange name; yet it fits so well. As the human race, we collectively need to work together in UNITY in order to save the Waters of our planet. The quality of Water affects every aspect of our lives… The enormity and importance of this statement is just beginning to be recognized by many of those in the forefront of Health and Healing research. It is essential for the long term survival of all who live on Mother Earth for the energetic integrity of our Water to be restored. People and our extensive activities have resulted in the pollution of the Waters… Now we need to UNITE in order to reverse this process.

*Unity Over Water*, by its very name, draws attention to this need for UNITY for us to work together, with ONE vision for the restoration of Divine Perfection upon the Earth.

This is also an Image Key to inspire TRUST.

*Unity Over Water* encourages us to trust the support of the Spiritual Hierarchy and the Astrological Alignments which are initiating this present expansion of spiritual development. *Unity Over Water* encourages us to TRUST so we can continue to spread UNCONDITIONAL LOVE and COMPASSION throughout the world!

During a meditation with *Unity Over Water*, King Arthur said to me,

> "We will succeed!
> We will get it RIGHT this time."

We are in the process of bringing Heaven to Earth in order to experience:

JOY, BEAUTY and PEACE.

# ArchAngel Metatron
## speaks* for Unity Over Water:

I AM
the Flower of Life Unlocked,
the Wisdom revealed.

I bring the Rainbow Rays
deep within your Heart and physical body,
activating and strengthening your physical systems.

My greatest joy is to see the stirrings within you as you begin
to accelerate your awakening...
begin to feel more ALIVE... begin to connect with your JOY.

My job is to trigger your own sense of KNOWING...
How does it feel within your HEART when you sense that something is TRUTH?

Many have come before this time to demonstrate the principals
of UNCONDITIONAL LOVE, COMPASSION and PEACE.

NOW is the opportunity for ALL to experience this,
fully supported by the energies of the Universe.

This is a time like no other.
We will get it "right" this time...
We will succeed in bringing the energies of HEAVEN
into the experience of LIFE ON EARTH.

Release your FEARS of the PAST
and enjoy the JOURNEY.

*as channelled by Barbara Evans

# Mary Magdalene
## speaks* for Unity Over Water:

UNITY…
is the perfect combination of
Divine Feminine
with Divine Masculine energies.

Their gifts intertwine to reveal
the Wisdom of Creation.

The UNITY SYMBOL
holds the geometry of this perfect union…

It is nurturing and supportive,
active and expanding.

Restoring the Life Force within the Waters is vital
to survival upon the EARTH,
vital to your HEALTH and Well-being.

Restoring the Divine Feminine energies of Creation
to their place of perfect UNION
within this physical realm
is a priority
for successful transformation.

*as channelled by Barbara Evans

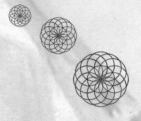

# #3 Gift of the Feminine

*THREE… a Trinity… Three… a Celebration…*

THREE… *Gift of the Feminine* focuses on three gifts…
Creativity, Grace and Intuition.

These three gifts automatically lead us to celebration and
gratitude within our being and within our life.

Once fully activated within us,
these gifts overflow through us into the rest of the world.

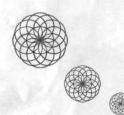

# Gift of the Feminine
## Image Key #3

Affirmation #3

I ALLOW creativity, grace and intuition to awaken within.

# *Gift of the Feminine*

Poem #3

With gentle beauty and quiet strength

the gifts of the feminine

are awakened within...

Creativity, Grace and Intuition.

Decree #3

**I AM Creative, Intuitive and filled with Grace.**

# Gift of the Feminine
## Image Key #3

## I AM Creative, Intuitive and filled with Grace.

G*ift of the Feminine* came immediately after the completion of *Unity Over Water*... That initial flow of inspiration was still powerful within my Being. The guidance was to draw the Genesis Pattern in feminine form.

I knew this energy was required for my own healing. It partnered with the image, *Crystal Wheel*, drawn in June of 2003... The *Crystal Wheel* is the masculine form of this same geometry and is the background Image for the Introduction to this book.

Seven circles come together within the Genesis Pattern forming three distinct areas... six inner "lotus" petals, six larger petals and six arcs around the outer perimeter.

1-Peridot
2-Zincite
3-Seraphinite
4-Zincite
5-Golden
  Topaz
6-Citrine
7-Garnet
8-Ruby
9-Garnet
10-Malachite
11-Chrysocolla
12-Ajoite
13-Lapis Lazuli
14-Sodalite

15-Azurite
16-Amethyst
17-Purple
  Fluorite
18-Modavite
19-Emerald
20-Tibetan
  Tektite
21-Petalite
22-Selenite
23-White
  Moldavite
24-Azeztulite
25-Selenite
26-Phenacite

*Gift of the Feminine*, stage one

The outer arcs were painted first, then the two large vertical petals. The crystals involved with this stage demonstrate the link between colors and crystals.

There are six clear, colorless crystals placed within the six inner "lotus" petals that contribute their vibrations to the center of the Image Key...

These are Phenacite, Petalite, Selenite, White Moldavite, Azeztulite and Selenite. At this stage of creation there is a resemblance to butterfly wings... a hint of the transformational possibilities which *Gift of the Feminine* holds.

As I worked, stones and crystals carrying feminine energies called to me to be included. This came as a strong knowing of which crystal energies I needed to weave, and exactly where their unique contribution should be channeled.

Within the photograph below, the second stage of the painting is complete. Again the relationship between colors within the Image Key and colors of the crystals is clearly seen.

1-Zincite
2-Peridot
3-Zincite
4-Pink Calcite
5-Pink Topaz
6-Kunzite
7-Rose Quartz

8-Chrysocolla
9-Ajoite
10-Prehnite
11-Green Apophyllite
12-Pink Lazurine
13-Ametrine

*Gift of the Feminine,* stage two

The crystals are aligned with the inner colored petals into which their energy was channelled. The outer arcs carry energies of crystals shown in stage one.

These two photographs also highlight how many crystals were involved with the creation of this relatively simple Image Key.

*"V" Symbol of the Feminine*

The white "lotus" petals at the center of *Gift of the Feminine* form a "V" shaped receptive cup. The position of these petals indicates the gender of the geometry.

Three Goddesses from two ancient civilizations stepped forward to guide and contribute to this Image Key: Isis, Hathor and Juno.

GOLD and SILVER are used to represent the Divine Masculine and Divine Feminine Energies.

Within *Gift of the Feminine* gold and silver interweave within the Genesis Pattern itself and within the background. Always there is feminine within the masculine and masculine within the feminine in order to create balance of these Divine energies.

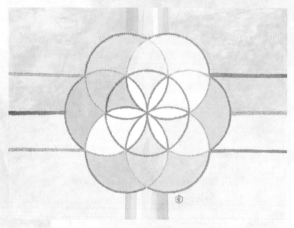

*Gold and Silver*

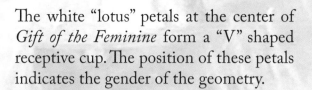

*Colors of the Peacock*

The olive green and turquoise blue of the background together with the two central vertical petals were inspired by the colors of a peacock tail feather... The peacock is often linked to both Isis and Juno.

The powerful rainbow seen with *Healing the Waters of the Earth* is repeated within *Gift of the Feminine*...

The rainbow facilitates connection to the Heart of the Universe and the Heart of the Earth... The rainbow supports our connection to SOURCE and our ability to fully ground the new expanding energies into our physical Being and the Earth.

*Rainbow*

As progress on the painting continued, I became increasingly aware of how much I personally needed the transformational energies offered by *Gift of the Feminine*. At the time I did not realize that my need to access and develop the feminine aspects of myself was a trend and concept growing rapidly within the spiritual community in general.

As I shared the completed painting with a friend, she drew my attention to the importance of fully awakening the Divine Feminine Energies upon the Earth and within Humanity.

From this point on, I began to notice increasing attention being paid to the return of the Divine Feminine Energies with emphasis on their vital role in the evolution and ascension of Humanity.

*Gift of the Feminine* took her place as Image Key #3. This is not just an Image Key for those within a female body in this lifetime. We all have both masculine and feminine aspects within us. It is as important for the males of our world to develop and nurture these feminine gifts, as it is for the females to RECLAIM them... In both males and females, this represents an awakening of dormant energies... The masculine and feminine energies are the Twin Flames within our Being... Their full activation and balance are essential for our experience of wholeness and well-being.

For eons, since the time of the ancient civilization called Lemuria, there has been a tendency for the feminine gifts to be suppressed and devalued throughout the world... This imbalance has contributed to the development of severe problems which have been prevalent in so many societies throughout the 2000 plus years of the Piscean Age.

In order for each of us to reach our full potential, and for world communities to regain their balance, the masculine and feminine energies need to be equally honored through CHOICE.

This restoration of the Balance of Masculine and Feminine energies can only take place by Choice... a choice which begins at the level of the individual. As balanced individuals within our families and communities, we then have the ability to offer these wonderful gifts for the benefit of all.

As we honor these gifts, they become an active part of our Being. The gifts create a flow, through which we are able to make different and more compassionate choices for ourselves, for Humanity and for the Earth herself. Life becomes easier for all.

*Gift of the Feminine* is a beautiful Image Key for young children as it assists them to maintain and develop their innate capabilities of creativity and intuition. Much of children's creativity is suppressed in this world. This all too often presents harsh experience and harsh environments within their young and impressionable lives.

*Gift of the Feminine* is an Image Key of gentle beauty and quiet strength. It carries Love and Joy into the center of your HEART, awakening dormant parts of yourself and encouraging a sense of Wholeness.

# ArchAngel Metatron
## speaks* for Gift of the Feminine:

I AM
the creative energy of
the Divine Feminine.

I AM here to inspire your creativity and intuition
by powerfully connecting
with your creative and intuitive centers.

I stimulate your connections to the Divine Energies
that power these feminine gifts within all who choose to accept them.

My joy is to see you grow and begin to flow with these creative juices…
for you are all Divine Creators…
You all have this ability within you.

My job is to inspire you.
My geometry is simple.
In the simplicity lies my power.

I invite you to accept this invitation and draw my energy into your Being.

Hold it within your MIND,
your HEART
and your CREATIVE CENTER just below the navel.

I ask you to accept with GRATITUDE
the awakening of your
Divine Feminine energies.

*as channelled by Barbara Evans

# Mary Magdalene
## speaks* for Gift of the Feminine:

The female version of
the Geometry of Creation…
in its simplicity…
is imbued with a touch of Crystal
LOVE and LIGHT.

Divine Feminine energies activate
your intuition and creativity…

This creativity comes via the HEART,
and is filled with LOVE and COMPASSION for ALL LIFE.

By ALL LIFE
I include
the animals and plants,
crystals and rocks,
Devas and Elementals,
together with the WATERS of your Mother Earth…
in addition to your fellow humans.

Creativity through
LOVE and COMPASSION
is the Divine Feminine way.
It is strong and powerful,
deeply rooted within the very HEART
of the EARTH herself.

*as channelled by Barbara Evans

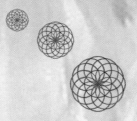

# #4 Labyrinth of Crystal Light

*FOUR... the World of Form and Manifestation...*

FOUR... *Labyrinth of Crystal Light* leads us
to the awareness of life
as a sacred and supported journey.

Life is a journey of physical form in which we interact with all
things physical. As we walk we are supported by the spiritual
beings of Love and Light who constantly surround us.

*Labyrinth of Crystal Light* calls
us to REMEMBER.

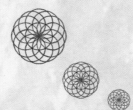

# Labyrinth of Crystal Light
## Image Key #4

## Affirmation #4

I ALLOW myself to walk this sacred and supported path.

# Labyrinth of Crystal Light

Poem #4

As I chose to walk this Sacred path

Remembering the true vastness of my being,

I ALLOW myself to be supported.

I ALLOW myself to awaken to the

wholeness and full potential of my Divine Self.

Decree #4

**I AM fully supported upon this Sacred Path.**

# Labyrinth of Crystal Light
## Image Key #4

## I AM fully supported upon this sacred path.

Labyrinths have been dear to my heart since reading *The Ancient Secret of the Flower of Life* by Drunvalo Melchizedek in the Fall of 1999. The small seven fold labyrinth within those pages caught my attention. The labyrinth has continued to hold a special place within my heart and knowing.

With three Image Keys complete and still no real sense of the enormity of the commitment that was opening before and within me, I knew it was time to revisit the labyrinth and bring it into this series of paintings.

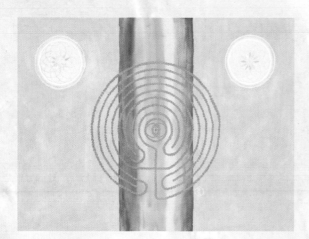

*Labyrinth of Crystal Light* is a seven fold labyrinth. There are seven layers to the pathway leading into and out of the center. Unlike a maze, you cannot become lost in a Labyrinth. Once you enter the pathway of the Labyrinth you are guided to the center...

**Labyrinth**
with its Rainbow of Crystal Light

The folds of the Labyrinth are numbered from 1-7 beginning at the outermost fold of the pathway.

There is a correspondence through the numbers to the seven major energy centers of the human energy body.

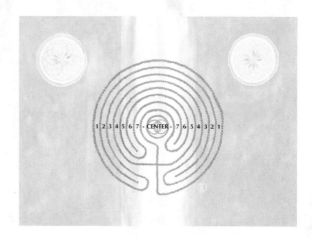

**Labyrinth Layers by Chakras**

On the occasions I have walked a labyrinth I have been guided to sit upon the ground within this central place... feeling the peace and connection to ALL THAT IS.

The center is a place to ALLOW, a place to quiet the mind and fully experience the sacredness and connection this sacred center offers.

My guidance suggests this central position corresponds to the SOUL STAR CHAKRA which is found within the energy body several inches above the crown of the head.

A Vesica Piscis is found at the Heart of *Labyrinth of Crystal Light*. As outlined on page 10, a Vesica Piscis is formed when two circles overlap so that the outer edge of each passes through the central point of the other circle. The inner "almond" shape is the actual Vesica.

*"Labyrinth of Crystal Light" Vesica Piscis*
with Diamond and Cross

Within this Image Key there is a diamond inside the Vesica... This is seen more easily within the illustration where the diamond is drawn in orange. The points of the diamond touch the central point of each circle together with the upper and lower intersecting points. This diamond is a symbol representing the 5th dimension.

Inside the diamond there is a cross, yellow in the illustration. This connects the points of the diamond and marks the length and breadth of the Vesica.

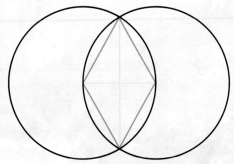

*Illustration of Vesica Piscis*
with Diamond and Cross

The labyrinth within *Labyrinth of Crystal Light* guides you to the center to contemplate the geometry of creation and the symbol of the 5th dimension...the Vesica Piscis and diamond. The simple shape of Vesica Piscis is one of the most sacred symbols in existence. Within this sacred space you are invited to ALLOW yourself to be fully supported on your life's journey. Once the period of contemplation and prayer within the center feels complete, the Labyrinth's path awaits to lead you out... back through the sequence of folds and chakras... back into everyday life.

As you sit with *Labyrinth of Crystal Light* before you, you may "walk" this pathway using a finger to guide your way. Alternatively, you may prefer to "walk" the pathway within your mind.

However you choose to experience this labyrinth, notice that you are "walking" through the colors, chakras and crystaline energies anchored into the painting during its creation. You are weaving through the healing, energizing vibrations of all the rainbow colors, together with the crystaline energies of Garnet, Carnelian, Citrine, Aventurine, Aquamarine, Lapis Lazuli and Amethyst. These vibrations support the manifestation of this spiritual journey into form, offering the energy of the Universe… which is both energizing and healing to help us on our spiritual journey.

As you enter the labyrinth you are entering the domain of the 3rd Chakra… the solar plexus, area of self esteem and personal power…

Following the pathway naturally leads you into the 2nd fold relating to the 2nd Chakra… our connection to creativity on all levels.

The motion is flowing as we are then led into the outermost fold corresponding to the 1st Chakra… safety, family and our place in this world…

Next we are guided into the 4th fold… the area of the HEART and Heart Chakra… our ability to connect with and experience LOVE, JOY and GRATITUDE… The movement is graceful… Beauty and grace touch deeply within every aspect of our Being…

The next step of the journey leads us into the 7th fold… The 7th Chakra is our Crown Chakra… connection to our Divine Self and Highest Guidance…

At this point we are close to the center, yet the pathway draws us outwards once more in order to enter the 6th fold… The gifts of the 6th Chakra are intuition and insight…

Again we head outwards as we enter the final fold of the entry phase… the 5th fold… representing the 5th Chakra which offers the gift of communciation, our ability to communicate with others… the path flows on…

NOW we arrive at the CENTER of the Labyrinth… the inward journey complete…

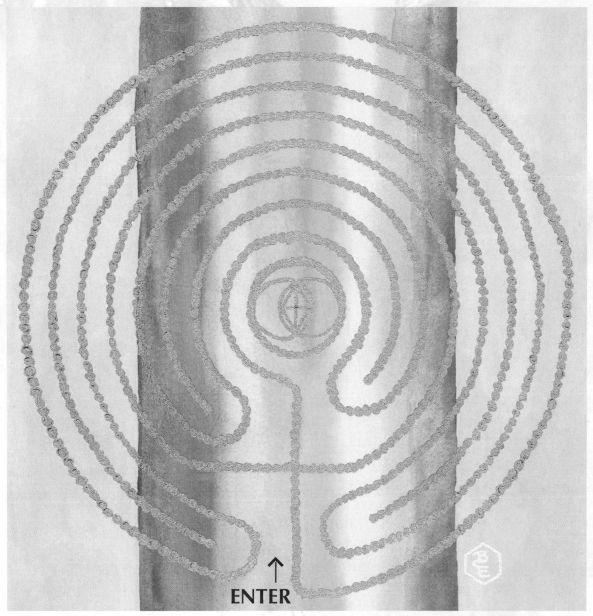

**ENTER**

*Magnified Labyrinth*
an Invitation to Finger Walk

There is a process of balancing taking place throughout this journey to the CENTER. Balancing enhances our connection to Spirit, our own spiritual self and our spirit guides. Our ability to feel the sacredness of the center is activated during the inward journey so that as we arrive, contemplation and prayer come very naturally... We are connected to Spirit and to our HEART WISDOM.

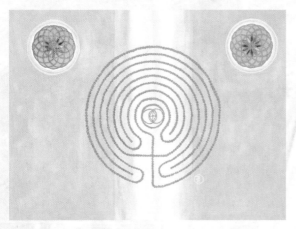

*Labyrinth and Unity Symbols*

On either side of the Labyrinth is a golden Unity Symbol… These Unity symbols are like two suns radiating their energy upon the Labyrinth. Their central lotus petals reflect the rainbow colors. Together the Unity symbols and Labyrinth form a downward pointing triangle. The triangle is symbolic of sacred knowledge within the sacred energy being transmitted from Heaven to Earth.

During the co-creation of this Image Key, I invoked the presence of two guides. First, I called Nematona into the left side as you look at the Image Key… She is a Goddess of circles, labyrinths and sacred ceremonies. The crystal associated with this side of the Image Key is Charoite… Charoite is a crystal that stimulates one's awareness and connection to the path of service each of us chose and committed to before entering this incarnation.

*Charoite on Quartz*

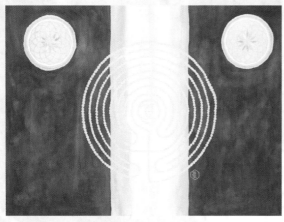

*Purple Background*

When I study the purple… Nematona becomes visible… Next to Nematona is a man who identifies himself as Enoch. Enoch is said to have become ArchAngel Metatron… So, within this Image Key, an ArchAngel appears in the form he lived as a human.

I knew very little about Enoch when painting *Labyrinth of Crystal Light*… Since then I have found *The Book of*

*Knowledge: The Keys of Enoch* by J. J. Hurtak. I now realize the significance of his presence in this particular Image Key. It is a great honor. Enoch works for the evolution of our Earth and of Humanity from a high place within the Spiritual Hierarchy. In addition, I now recognize ArchAngel Metatron as the over-lighting guide for all of the Image Keys being co-created and manifested through me.

The second guide to be called into the Image Key is Lleu, a Sun God of Ancient Britain, together with his magical hound. Both Lleu and his hound can be seen blessing this work within the purple of the right hand side. I was drawn to call upon Lleu due to his obvious connection to the sun and more subtle connection to labyrinths. The crystal energy accompanying Lleu is Amethyst, which strengthens our ability to receive guidance.

We are all children of the Divine Creator… The path we walk on Earth is a sacred path. Once we begin to awaken and remember who we are, we become increasingly aware of how supported we are in every step we take. The more we ask for guidance and assistance the more those prayers are answered.

For many, this beautiful piece is the first of the Image Keys they feel a strong connection to, as its form is more familiar than the more complex geometry of the other Image Keys. It is a wonderful Image Key for children setting out on their new journey of life.

As we choose to acknowledge the sacredness of our journey, we begin to allow ourselves to awaken to the wholeness and full potential of our true Divine Self. *Labyrinth of Crystal Light* calls us to Remember.

# ArchAngel Metatron
## speaks* for Labyrinth of Crystal Light:

I AM the Wayshower,
illuminated by
Crystal Rainbow Light.

I AM here to show you that you cannot make a wrong turn
in this experience called LIFE.

All has the potential to lead you to the CENTER.
The CENTER is the realization that you are a CHILD
of the DIVINE CREATOR... and you are greatly LOVED.

Whatever choices you have made in the past, you are being invited NOW
to AWAKEN and choose UNCONDITIONAL LOVE and COMPASSION
as your foundations of LIFE.

My greatest joy is to see you say "Yes" and make that step and commitment
to find your TRUTH and MAGNIFICENCE, to find your JOY.
My job is to offer support as you walk this sacred and supported path.

NO ONE walks this path alone. All have loving guides right by their side…
ASK for their assistance if you would like their help.
ASK for their assistance if you feel LOST.
ASK for their assistance if you feel UNLOVED.
ASK for their assistance to find
FORGIVENESS and GRATITUDE.
BELIEVE that they can help,
express your GRATITUDE as you open
and begin to RECIEVE.

*as channelled by Barbara Evans

# Mary Magdalene
## speaks* Labyrinth of Crystal Light:

Circles
have often been associated
with the Divine Feminine way.

Here the labyrinth
leads you via a circular path
highlighting the prayers within your HEART...

Feel the prayers awaken within you...

Feel the connections to intuition and creativity within your HEART.

Feel and encourage
the Divine Feminine
to AWAKEN within your HEART
and within your life...

for she has been sleeping
for eons of Earth Time, and NOW,
is the time for her return.

*as channelled by Barbara Evans

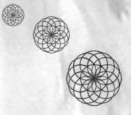

# #5 Harmonic Concordance

*FIVE... Inspires us to Change and Transform...*

FIVE... *Harmonic Concordance* is connected to
the burst of energy that occurred when six planets aligned
into a perfect six-pointed star
in November 2003.

This event has come to be known as the Harmonic Concordance.
The major essence of *Harmonic Concordance* is Evolution and
Transformation.

This astrological alignment is one example of
the great order and detail
within the Universe and its Divine Plan.

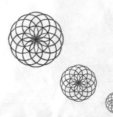

# Harmonic Concordance
## Image Key #5

## Affirmation #5

I ALLOW and embrace the Energy of Evolution
as it enters my Being.

# *Harmonic Concordance*

Poem #5

Spiritual Evolution is brought to Earth.

I open to new possibilities:

Unity, Balance and Evolution.

Awareness Awakens;

Evolution Integrates.

Decree #5

**I AM evolving with Balance and Grace.**

# *Harmonic Concordance*
## *Image Key #5*

## I AM evolving with Balance and Grace.

*Harmonic Concordance* represents an important leap in the creation of the Image Keys. It is the first Image Key to be consciously associated with an astrological alignment of the planets.

As friends started sending me E-mails about the upcoming event within the sky... my knowing was activated... I "knew" I was being guided to connect with this energy... like a translator, to receive the invisible energy in one form... then to translate it into visible form on paper. This allows others to see, feel and interact with the energy even after the planets have moved out of their special alignment.

Working with *Harmonic Concordance* opened me to a new awareness. These special energies and energy alignments penetrate every aspect of our world, whether we are aware and recognize them or not. It is however, easier for us, and we benefit more, if we consciously choose to be aware, active and involved.

If we are conscious of the new energies, they offer opportunities for us to accept and integrate them into deeper levels of our core being, with far more grace and ease than might otherwise be the case. By this active interaction and integration, we greatly assist our own evolution towards fully remembering our true Wholeness.

My role is to translate this and other similar events into a physical, visual form. People are then able to work with the gifts offered long after the astrological event has occurred... It is possible to assist the full integration of energies years after the astrological alignment.

The crystal energy at the HEART of this Image Key is Ajoite... It is a rare crystal that helps us to connect to the heart of the Earth and the heart of the Great Central Sun at the center of our Universe. There is a photograph of a small Ajoite crystal on page 12. This was my first piece of Ajoite.

As we focus on the geometry, we again see the Unity Symbol placed at the center of the Flower of Life. Within *Harmonic Concordance* the Flower of Life represents all potential and connection to ONENESS… the knowing we are all ONE… We are all connected to all that exists.

*Flower of Life and Unity Symbol*

A silver six-pointed star lies between the outer circles of the Flower of Life and a hexagon carrying the vibrations of a stone known as Healer's Gold.

The Star is composed of two interlocking triangles. The triangle pointing downwards in this Image Key represents the knowledge and power of spirit being transferred to this physical world at the time of the Harmonic Concordance. The upward pointing triangle represents Humanity as we strive to create Heaven on Earth.

*Six-Pointed Silver Star*
Inside a Hexagon of Healer's Gold

The six-pointed star also represents the Divine Masculine energies in their highest form. The star repeats the pattern formed in the sky by the alignment of six major planets at the time of the Harmonic Concordance… Each point represents the position of one of the planets. Such perfect geometric planetary alignments are relatively rare and signify special energetic moments.

*Planetary Alignment*
at the time of the Harmonic Concordance

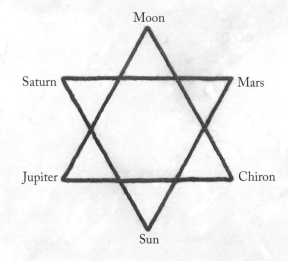

*African Gray Herderite and Golden Herderite*
resting on Quartz

The crystal energy within the silver star is African Gray Herderite, a crystal which encourages evolution.

The vibrations of Golden Herderite are found within the golden lotus petals at the center of the Unity Symbol seen in the illustration at the top of page 77.

The Hexagon, the six sided inner shape within *Harmonic Concordance,* represents both the Icosahedron and the Dodecahedron.

An Icosahedron has twenty sides, with each side being an equilateral triangle.

A Dodecahedron has twelve sides with each side being a pentagon. In a cross section, however, both can look like a six sided Hexagon.

The Icosahedron and Dodecahedron are Platonic Solids described and defined by Mathematics. Since the time of Plato, these two Platonic Solids have been associated with the Elements, Water and Ether.

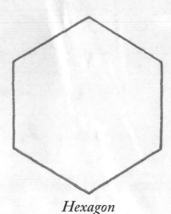

*Hexagon*

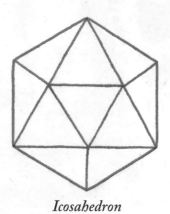

*Icosahedron*

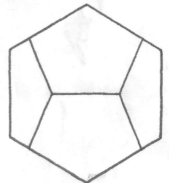

*Dodecahedron*

Within the human body the Water Element connects to the heart and emotional system. The Element Ether connects to spirit and to spiritual transformation.

Vibrations of Healers Gold are found within the Hexagon. Healers Gold is a combination of Magnetite and Pyrite and carries powerful healing energy. It also assists with the integration of high frequency healing energy into the physical body.

*Hexagon*

The yellow circle represents the sun from which rays of golden sunshine burst forth as the six points of the star touch its circumference.

Beyond the sunbursts is a background of rainbow light and crystal energies offering nourishment to our energetic body.

*Sun and Rainbow Colors of "2012 Cross"*

During a recent trip to England, I was introduced to Mick Twyman at The Shell Grotto in Margate. The walls of the Shell Grotto are covered in ancient mosaics made of local shells. For the last eight years Mick has been translating the incredible stories held within these mosaics.

A frequent pattern of the mosaics is a diagonal cross which Mick refers to as the "2012 Cross". I felt a powerful connection from deep within my being to this very sacred place and a recognition of Truth within the information we were privileged to receive.

As I laid the Image Keys out upon the floor of the area known as the Temple, *Harmonic Concordance* caught Mick's attention. After careful measurement he informed me that

*The Temple,*
*Margate Shell Grotto*

the angles within *Harmonic Concordance* exactly match those of the 2012 cross which he had described.

*Enlarged Orb,*
from photo on previous page

After receiving permission to place the 13 Image Keys in a circle upon the temple floor, this orb appeared in a sequence of photographs taken at the Temple.

Geometric patterns can be seen within this bright orb which moved around the circle as if studying different Image Keys. Additional fainter orbs are also present within some of the other photographs taken that day.

The energy of *Harmonic Concordance* is the energy of the Divine… of Heaven coming down to Earth. It is important to ground this energy… important to hold it within our physical reality so that the opportunity to integrate its precious gifts can be accepted by many as they make the choice to evolve into the New Golden Age… an Age of PEACE and BALANCE… of experiencing Heaven on Earth.

# ArchAngel Metatron
## speaks* for Harmonic Concordance:

I AM
Evolution in ACTION.

I bring the Divine Energies of Evolution
from the Higher Dimensions
into the physical plane of Earth.

I offer you a great opportunity to grow and evolve
through accepting my assistance.

The golden yellow light represents the rays of the SUN
interspersed by the Rainbow Rays...
you are bathed in my creative light of Evolution.

My greatest joy is to see your LIGHT ignite within you,
connecting your awareness to ALL THAT IS.
My job is to assist you to reach and fulfill your potential.

There have been many times when the masculine energies
have been distorted and out of balance.
The Divine Masculine Energies within this Image Key
are aligned with the ONE CREATOR.

This Image Key brings the Divine Masculine energies to Earth
in a balanced form to pave the way for the full
BALANCE of DIVINE MASCULINE
and DIVINE FEMININE
ENERGIES.

*as channelled by Barbara Evans

# Mary Magdalene
## speaks* Harmonic Concordance:

The importance
of this Image Key
is...
the introduction of the codes
of the
Divine Masculine Energies.

UNITY
is the combination of the
Divine Masculine and Divine Feminine,
both in their form of
PERFECTION.

This Image Key
restores and prepares the way,
an important role
in the return of UNITY
upon the Earth,
and by so doing,
facilitates
the process
of Spiritual Evolution.

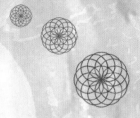

# #6 Galactic Connection

*SIX... Comes to me as the Number of God...*

SIX... the number of days in the story of Genesis
needed to complete the creation of Earth.

*Galactic Connection* links us back through the thinning veils
of forgetfulness to ALL THAT IS. *Galactic Connection*
creates within us the awareness of what has always been and
always will be…

*Galactic Connection* connects us
to the source
of ALL THAT IS…

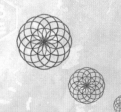

# *Galactic Connection*
## *Image Key #6*

## Affirmation #6

I ALLOW the awareness of Connections to ALL THAT IS.

# *Galactic Connection*

Poem #6

Music of the Spheres,

Awareness of Connections

to ALL THAT IS... Awaken.

Integration of the energies profound,

My energy expands.

Decree #6

**I AM ONE with All of Creation.**

# Galactic Connection
## *Image Key #6*

## I AM ONE with All of Creation.

The intensity I experienced between September and December 2003, when seven Image Keys were brought into physical form, was very new, exciting and certainly expansive to my own evolution… My life and understanding was changing rapidly.

***Central 12 Petal Lotus***
and Unity Symbol Overlay

Attention was drawn by my Spirit Guides to the concept of TWELVE surrounding the ONE. TWELVE surounding the ONE is a pattern already present within the Image Keys… as seen by the twelve petal lotus found at the center of the Unity Symbol… and the center of this Image Key.

I began to notice the theme of TWELVE surrounding the ONE elsewhere… Instances of this pattern can be found within the ancient traditions of many cultures. It is a concept increasingly present in metaphysical teachings of our time.

There is also increasingly more information coming from spiritual teachers about the expansion of our two stranded DNA into an advanced form of twelve strands… This is not something new, but rather a return towards our original DNA formation before we descended into such dense physical bodies.

The geometries were playing within my consciousness… A new Image Key was beginning to take shape. TWELVE surrounding the ONE is the concept behind *Galactic Connection.*

The geometry builds and expands upon the geometry of the earlier Image Keys. In the way the Unity Symbol was built by placing a Feminine Genesis Pattern over a Masculine Genesis Pattern, here the Double Flower of Life is built by placing a Feminine Flower of Life over a Masculine Flower of Life.

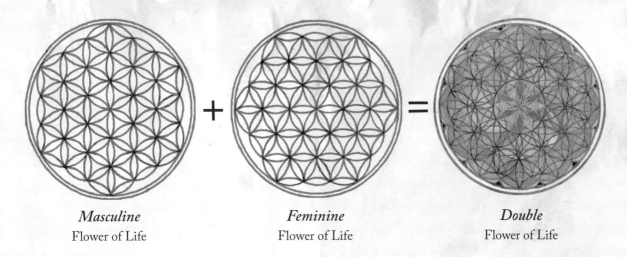

*Masculine*
Flower of Life

*Feminine*
Flower of Life

*Double*
Flower of Life

Masculine and Feminine energies are thus interwoven within this intricate pattern to create WHOLENESS and BALANCE.

This is the first Double Flower of Life I had drawn. It presented a considerable challenge requiring intense concentration… Every aspect of my being was involved as I stretched into the process… Rather than drawing or representing on paper the Double Flower of Life, it was as if I entered the geometric matrix itself.

My thoughts on the Flower of Life shifted as this work was being done. Previously I understood the Flower of Life to be a Universal Symbol recognized as a Blueprint for Creation throughout the Universe. Now I began to feel this expanded form… the Double Flower of Life … was even more important. It is as if the Flower of Life is offering the opportunity to discover this larger Blueprint. Furthermore, the traditional representation of the Flower of Life is with a double circle around the central geometry, reminding me now of the shell and membrane around a chicken's egg… protecting the perfection and potential held within.

A knowing developed… This double circle is similar to a seal: limiting the geometry, limiting our connection to the rest of the Universe, limiting our awareness of our own Higher Self.

Within *Galactic Connection* this seal is opened and once more our awareness is encouraged to develop and to form a clearer connection to our Higher Self, the rest of the Universe and to the ONE SOURCE of all creation.

The twelve golden discs found around the points of the twelve pointed star within *Galactic Connection* are also an important aspect of the Image Key...

The twelve-pointed star and twelve discs reflect expansiveness ... They take the geometry beyond the limits of the traditional double circle, beyond the seal.

*12 Golden Discs and 12-Pointed Star*

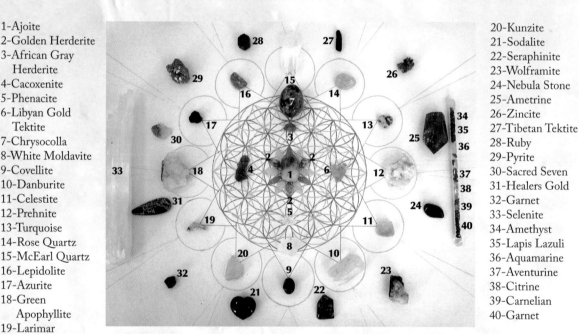

1-Ajoite
2-Golden Herderite
3-African Gray Herderite
4-Cacoxenite
5-Phenacite
6-Libyan Gold Tektite
7-Chrysocolla
8-White Moldavite
9-Covellite
10-Danburite
11-Celestite
12-Prehnite
13-Turquoise
14-Rose Quartz
15-McEarl Quartz
16-Lepidolite
17-Azurite
18-Green Apophyllite
19-Larimar

20-Kunzite
21-Sodalite
22-Seraphinite
23-Wolframite
24-Nebula Stone
25-Ametrine
26-Zincite
27-Tibetan Tektite
28-Ruby
29-Pyrite
30-Sacred Seven
31-Healers Gold
32-Garnet
33-Selenite
34-Amethyst
35-Lapis Lazuli
36-Aquamarine
37-Aventurine
38-Citrine
39-Carnelian
40-Garnet

*Galactic Connection Drawing with Crystals laid in Place*

Many crystals are involved with this Image Key. Their energies are interwoven with the dominant colors. Different crystals combine with the golden yellow of each disc resulting in each golden disc having its own signature and vibration.

Other crystals combine with the black and gold of Healers Gold forming the main area of the background.

Healers gold projects a feeling of Space and the Cosmos.

*Healers Gold*
Creates the Background

*Healers Gold on Quartz*

*Galactic Connection* stimulates and encourages the expansion of our consciousness. As this expansion of consciousness takes place, there is also stimulation and activation for the expansion of our DNA... *Galactic Connection* supports the reconnection and awakening of the full twelve stranded DNA compliment that is our heritage.

*Rainbow Rays*
Shooting into the Galaxy; guiding our Expansion

As connections are reawakened and reformed, we have the potential to become aware of the spiritual music of the spheres.

*Galactic Connection* is a powerful Image Key... It is an invitation to move beyond limitations that have been in place for eons of time. *Galactic Connection* is an invitation to expand our Conscious Awareness... a major step in realizing our full and true Potential.

# ArchAngel Metatron
## speaks* for Galactic Connection:

I AM
your ticket to Galactic Awareness.

I can help you remember and reconnect
your Awareness.

You have fully experienced separation
from GOD and from each other…
NOW it is time for you to be offered the opportunity
to remember that you are SO MUCH MORE.

You do have the ability to reawaken your connections
to all that exists
upon the Earth and out into the Galaxy, the Universe and the Cosmos.

My greatest joy is to feel you succeed.

Each step along the journey of awakening is a treasure
for you to enjoy and embrace.

My job is to activate your brain and DNA.

You are SO MUCH MORE than you tend to realize.

I invite and encourage you to
explore the possibilities
of your Vastness and your Greatness.

*as channelled by Barbara Evans

# Mary Magdalene
## speaks* for Galactic Connection:

Galactic Connection combines

the full Flower of Life

in Feminine and Masculine Form…

Feel the PERFECTION…

Feel the activations…

Feel the expansion this Image Key is offering to you NOW.


The Balance of the Divine Energies…

creating a Dance of Perfection to the

Music of the Spheres

as the energies stimulate all senses…

all possibilities.

*as channelled by Barbara Evans

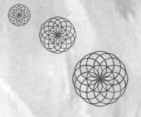

# #7 Crystal Visions

*SEVEN... a Sacred Number...*

I AM Crystal Clear.
My intentions,
My vision,
My Body, Mind and Spirit.

SEVEN... In many cultures
seven is held as a sacred number.

There are Native American Traditions which describe four directions... plus above, below and center... making seven. Eastern Traditions describe seven major chakras within our energy systems. There are seven circles within the Genesis Pattern. *Crystal Visions* is a very sacred piece as it holds the place of #7.

AS ABOVE, SO BELOW;
AS WITHIN, SO WITHOUT;
I AM CRYSTAL CLEAR, BODY, MIND and SOUL.

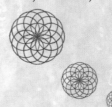

# Crystal Visions
## Image Key #7

Affirmation #7

I ALLOW love, balance and unity to BE my experience.

# *Crystal Visions*

## Poem #7

The Language of Light surrounds me,

Balance and Connection,

I am held in Divine Love.


## Decree #7

**I AM Crystal Clear.**

**...my Intentions,**

**...my Vision,**

**...my Body, Mind and Spirit.**

# Crystal Visions
## Image Key #7

## I AM Crystal Clear...
## my Intentions... my Vision... my Body, Mind and Spirit.

*Crystal Visions* holds the place of the seventh Image Key... It was the seventh to be completed, but not the seventh to be drawn... This Image Key was created in two distinct phases.

The story behind *Crystal Visions* begins shortly after the completion of *Healing the Waters of the Earth* and *Unity Over Water*. I was due to take these two original paintings on a road trip to three sacred sites in England... Stonehenge, Avebury and the Chalice Well in Glastonbury.

Before leaving I was guided to draw both *Gift of the Feminine* and *Crystal Visions*... Both drawings were within my portfolio as I traveled.

The geometry of *Crystal Visions* is the geometry of the UNITY SYMBOL.

*Quartz Crystal with Rainbows*

The colors within this Unity Symbol are inspired by the rainbows seen within a clear quartz crystal held to the light... the same crystal whose photo graces and creates the background of the pages before you.

This beautiful Rainbow Quartz Crystal has two smaller crystals partially embedded in one of its faces... These two smaller crystals are both "double terminated" with perfect terminations at either end.

In essence the crystal is a rainbow bridge between worlds. It is a teacher offering HOPE and JOY with this connection through the HEART.

The colors of the rainbow, like water, are essential to our health and well-being, essential to our survival on this planet.

As you bring your focus to the gold and silver filaments which form the structure of the Unity Symbol, you will find that the Male Genesis Pattern is golden and the Female Genesis Pattern is silver.

*Unity Symbol*

*Turquoise and Pink Center*

The central circle of the Unity Symbol is empowered by the vibrations of Ajoite, within the turquoise petals, and Kunzite, within the pink background.

*Kunzite Crystal*

Each of these crystals carry high quotients of LOVE, peace and tranquility.

The powerful energies within this Image Key act like a generator pulsing LOVE into any environment in which *Crystal Visions* is placed.

*Ajoite Crystal*

*Rainbow, Silver and Gold*

The vertical rainbow links the Unity Symbol to the heart of the Universe and the heart of the Earth. The rainbow assists us to ground the higher energies both into our physical body and into the Earth. The rainbow also supports smooth energy flow as we grow and transform.

The horizontal Gold and Silver bands represent the Golden Ray of Christ Consciousness and the Silver Ray of Grace and Compassion.

At this stage I felt *Crystal Visions* was complete... the background color remained WHITE! I began working on *Labyrinth of Crystal Light*, *Harmonic Concordance* and *Galactic Connection*, all the time feeling that *Crystal Visions* was complete. Suddenly after completing *Galactic Connection*... I received further inspiration and guidance... It was now time to paint the background of *Crystal Visions*.

*Crystal Visions, Stage 1*
White Background

This makes complete sense to me...

A message from Merlyn was channelled during a healing session I received. Merlyn explained that the Images I paint represent stages in the journey of my SOUL. As I move through the evolutionary steps and record them, others are able to use the Image Keys to assist their own unique soul journey.

So although I was ready to complete *Crystal Visions* to the point of stage one, I needed to make the further evolutionary steps represented in *Harmonic Concordance* and *Galactic Connection* before bringing through the first "Gold and Silver Squiggles" into the Image Keys.

The "Gold and Silver Squiggles" represent the LANGUAGE OF LIGHT.

As the four colors were painted and infused with crystal energies, I was guided to connect them with four groups of Galactic Healers of the Seventh Dimension or higher. Later as the Language of Light symbols were channeled, the same connections were made. The connection for silver on green was to Healers of Andromeda. Silver on red connects to Healers from Venus… Andromeda and Venus represent and support the Feminine energies within this Image Key. For the purple and gold the connection is with Healers of Arcturus.

*Language of Light Symbols with Connections* to Andromeda, Venus, Arcturus and Chiron

The blue and gold connects with Healers of Chiron… Arcturus and Chiron represent and support the Masculine energies within this Image Key.

*Crystal Visions* is yet another major step on the journey of the Image Keys due to the inclusion of the channeled Symbols representing the Language of Light.

I was also guided to include the following words…

AS ABOVE, SO BELOW;

AS WITHIN, SO WITHOUT.

The words AS ABOVE, SO BELOW are attributed to The Emerald Tablets and to Hermes Trimegistus… combining the wisdom of the Egyptian God Thoth and the Greek God Hermes.

This is an Image Key to aid with developing clarity on all levels…

CLARITY OF BODY, MIND AND SPIRIT.

# ArchAngel Metatron
## speaks* for Crystal Visions:

*I AM the Crystal Clear
Vibrations of LOVE and LIGHT.*

*I can help you to find your own clarity,
clear the lower energies
and find your own crystal clear LIGHT,
so that it can shine through for all to see.*

*My greatest joy is the play of LIGHT and LOVE as they intertwine
to touch your Life and HEART, awakening the Joy deep within you.*

*My job is awakener, AWAKENER…
I awaken you to the beauty that you are.*

*Many within the Universe are supporting this evolution on Earth.
It is a great experiment within the Cosmos…
All are watching… Many are assisting.*

*You are invited to recognize them and their existence beyond the Earth.*

*Accept their support.*

*This evolution and awakening is not something
to be achieved in isolation…
It is to BE by recognition of one's role
within the WHOLE OF CREATION…*

*ONE'S recognition of
ALL THAT IS.*

*as channelled by Barbara Evans

# Mary Magdalene
## speaks* for Crystal Visions:

The central circle of Crystal Visions

radiates LIQUID LOVE...

pulsing LOVE out into the environment...

LOVE flowing in never ending expansion.


UNITY is again presented before you...

UNITY of the Divine Masculine and Divine Feminine energies...

inviting you to awaken

the UNITY within you.


Awaken the long forgotten Divinity

that you are

as a child of the Divine Creator.

*as channelled by Barbara Evans

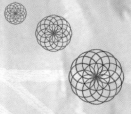

# #8 Return of the Feminine

*EIGHT... 8 becomes ∞ the Sign of Infinity...*

EIGHT... The pastel petals of this Feminine Flower of Life
flow like repeating infinity symbols across the page.

The return of the Divine Feminine energy is a vital piece,
missing for so long from much of our world... key to our
future, our survival, our very existence as a species upon planet
Earth.

∞ Infinity... perfect for *Return of the Feminine* ∞
8 Taking us to the next level 8

# *Return of the Feminine*
## *Image Key #8*

## Affirmation #8

# I ALLOW the Divine Feminine to activate within.

# Return of the Feminine

Poem #8

Powerfully the Divine Feminine Returns to Earth,

Messages of light within the petals found...

With gratitude, the blessings enter my being.

Decree #8

**I AM dancing in the Light of the Divine Feminine.**

# Return of the Feminine
## Image Key #8

## I AM dancing in the light of the Divine Feminine.

*Return of the Feminine* was created over the 2004 Easter Weekend together with Image Key #9, *Resurrection and Balance*.

Both *Return of the Feminine* and *Resurrection and Balance* are inspired and guided by Mary Magdalene.

I had felt a strong connection to Mary Magdalene for several years. Now I was being guided to connect with her more fully. To facilitate this process I laid out a special Crystal Grid within my studio which I called the "Mary Magdalene Grid". I then entered the grid and placed a vase of fresh roses within the very sacred space.

*Polished Eudialyte*

Mary Magdalene is frequently associated with a Rose, often a Blue Rose. Personally, I also feel the connection to her through Magenta Roses. I always think of her and feel her presence when I see a magenta colored rose. Mary Magdalene is also associated with the Rose Line, a major energy line within the Earth that travels from Compostela de Santiago in Northern Spain to the Island of Orkney in Scotland. The Rose Line is not drawn upon the surface of the Earth. It is purely energetic in form.

I meditated within the sacred space of the "Mary Magdalene Grid"... calling upon Mary Magdalene to be present. I became aware of powerful energies moving throughout my being... particularly strong around the crown of my head... I felt the connection to Mary Magdalene and knew that all was in Divine Order.

A new crystal called Eudialyte was part of this "Mary Magdalene Grid".

This particular piece of Eudialyte has continued to be an important crystal assisting me to connect with Mary Magdalene's energy throughout the remaining Image Keys... a beautiful, yet powerful crystal of the Magenta Ray.

If you study the surface of the Eudialyte within the photograph on the previous page, you may find her face revealed to you in the upper left hand corner of the stone.

*Horizontal Petals*

The Geometry of *Return of the Feminine* is the Flower of Life in Feminine form... in which the petals cross the page in horizontal bands.

Within these silver horizontal petals are found golden symbols representing the Language of Light.

*Language of Light*

Though the geometry is comparatively simple, the experience of bringing this Image Key into Being was very intense... To me, this indicates the strength with which the Divine Feminine energies are returning to the Earth at this time.

This power is also reflected by the intensity of the background colors representing both the Rainbow Rays and the colors of the Major Energy Centers of the body.

*Background Colors*

This powerful return of the Feminine Energies is vital in order to create UNITY and BALANCE with the Masculine Energies. The Feminine Energies are returning in order to co-create HARMONY… There is no intent to replace the Masculine Energies, but rather to Balance and combine with them in a perfect relationship… to bring PEACE upon Earth.

It is therefore an essential step in the evolution of Humanity for the Divine Feminine Energies to be accepted and integrated within every level of life… within each individual, whether male or female, within family, society and global community. It is important for the gifts of the Masculine energies and the gifts of the Feminine energies to be recognized and honored by all.

*Polished Lemurian Quartz*

*Citrine Sphere*

*Selenite Sphere*

*Red Cap Amethyst*

*Fluorite with Yytrium*

*Lapis Lazuli*

*Hackmanite*

*Prehnite*

*Green Apophyllite*

*Watermelon Tourmaline*  *Aquarian Presence*  *Pink Tourmaline*

**Return of the Feminine**
with Twelve Crystals from the Grid used for its Creation

These two Image Keys were created at my studio in New York on the very same week-end Tom Kenyon and Judy Sion were holding a conclave near Washington D.C. They were anchoring the Divine Feminine Energies into that important area. Tom Kenyon does amazing Sound Healing work with Mary Magdalene... frequently channeling her singing voice, together with that of Jeshua.

*Return of the Feminine* is here to assist with the awakening, acceptance and integration of the Divine Feminine Energies... to ease our way with this most exciting and necessary process.

Mary Magdalene, as representative of the Feminine aspect of Christ Consciousness, adds her blessing to this Image Key.

# ArchAngel Metatron
## speaks* for Return of the Feminine:

I AM a message direct
from the Divine Mother.

I AM encoded with LOVE and LIGHT
that will trigger within you the activation
of the Divine Feminine energies.

My greatest joy is to see and feel and know that the
Divine Feminine Energies are activating upon the Earth
after so long a period of Earth History.
My job is to assist with this powerful return and activation
of the Divine Feminine.
Without the Feminine presence in full glory,
there can only be imbalance and distress.

I come to address this imbalance and lead the way
to PEACE and HARMONY with ABUNDANCE for ALL.
All over the World the Divine Feminine Energies are awakening.

This Image Key is here to ease the way,
to gracefully assist the integration into every level of LIFE and experience.
It is a powerful return.
It is a powerful Image Key, yet it is also gentle in its unfolding.

Again you are invited to fully experience the WONDER
that is available to you...
the wonder that
you ARE.

*as channelled by Barbara Evans

# Mary Magdalene
## *speaks\* for Return of the Feminine:*

This is the first of
my signature Image Keys…

the first time Barbara truly called upon me,

Mary Magdalene,

to assist her with her work.

We had connected before,

but this is our first major collaboration
within this lifetime.

Feel the shift that takes place as you work with this Image Key.

Feel the Blessings of the Divine Mother

as they are offered
for your acceptance.

\*as channelled by Barbara Evans

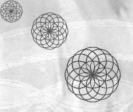

# #9 Resurrection and Balance

*NINE... is about Completion...*

NINE... Within *Resurrection and Balance*
we find the Masculine Flower of Life
together with the Feminine Flower of Life, connecting
to create the Unity Symbol...
the Holy Child... the Holy Grail.

The coming together of the Masculine and Feminine energies
in perfect balance to create the Divine Child is most definitely
one level of completion... a level of completion that opens the
way for new beginnings.

# *Resurrection and Balance*
## *Image Key #9*

## Affirmation #9

I ALLOW the activation and integration of
Divine Masculine and Divine Feminine within my Being.

# *Resurrection and Balance*

Poem #9

The Divine Masculine combines

with the Divine Feminine creating

Perfect UNITY and BALANCE...

The Holy Grail,

The Holy Child.

Decree #9

**I AM Unity and Balance within;**

**I AM a Child of the Divine Creator.**

# Resurrection and Balance
## Image Key #9

## I AM Unity and Balance within;
## I AM a Child of the Divine Creator.

Second of the "Mary Magdalene" Image Keys, *Resurrection and Balance*, takes the journey to the next stage.

*Return of the Feminine* focuses on the return of the Divine Feminine Energies together with their acceptance and integration.

*Resurrection and Balance* combines within its geometry the Divine Masculine and Divine Feminine Energies… blending these energies in complete balance to bring forth the Divine Child… here represented by the Unity Symbol.

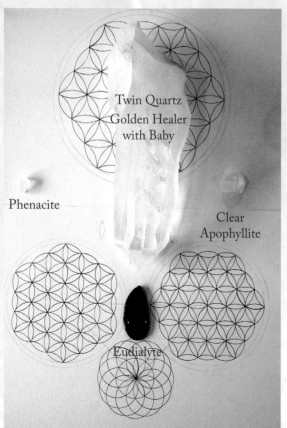

Twin Quartz
Golden Healer
with Baby

Phenacite

Clear
Apophyllite

Eudialyte

The two Image Keys are shown just after their drawings were completed. *Return of the Feminine* is above and *Resurrection and Balance* below… Highlighting the connection and flow between the two is a large quartz crystal.

The small colorless crystal on the left is Phenacite… a powerful stone of initiation. The crystal on the right is Clear Apophyllite which I consider to be very angelic… helping us to connect to the higher realms.

The large crystal in the center mirrors the concept of *Resurrection and Balance*… It consists of a trinity of Father, Mother and Child.

*Drawings with Crystals*

As you look carefully at this large crystal, you see it is composed of two fused crystal points lying side by side... This is referred to as a "twin". Near the base there is a third baby crystal. As I look at the crystal... the male and female energies are represented by the Twins; the baby crystal represents the Divine Child. There is also a faint golden hue to parts of the crystal, paticularly around the "child", so it is called a Golden Healer.

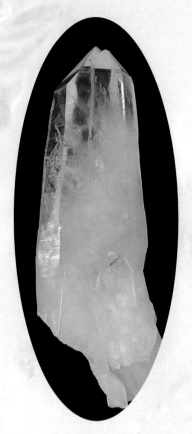

*Twin Quartz Golden Healer*
with baby crystal

Looking at the geometry in more detail...

*Divine Masculine*

The Masculine Flower of Life on the left hand side of the Image Key has petals running vertically through the Geometry.

The Feminine Flower of Life on the right has its petals flowing horizontally.

As with many of the other Image Keys... Gold is used to symbolize Masculine Energies and Silver is used to represent Feminine Energies.

*Divine Feminine*

*Magenta Triangle*

A Magenta Triangle springs from the most central point of each Flower of Life... connecting the two in Sacred Union. This Magenta triangle represents the Chalice, Womb or Holy Grail... It points downwards to indicate Divine Energies being brought to Earth.

Eudialyte crystal energy is held within the Magenta Triangle anchoring the blessings of Mary Magdalene into the Image key.

The lowest point of the Magenta Triangle touches the heart of the Unity Symbol... the Heart of the Divine Child. Here, the Masculine and Feminine Energies are in perfect Balance with interweaving filaments of silver and gold.

*Divine Child*

*Helix*

A descending helix represents the Divine DNA Blueprint of Humanity spiraling into this sacred chalice. Below the Unity Symbol the helix continues and represents the anchoring of these Divine Energies into our lives and into the fabric of our planet.

Above each Flower of Life is a small petal...
These petals represent drops of sacred
elixir, Gold for the Divine Masculine and
Silver for the Divine Feminine.

Imagine these sacred elixers are flowing
into the geometry below them.

The photograph below displays the
Signature Crystals for *Resurrection and
Balance* resting upon the areas where they
are most powerfully aligned.

*Petals of Sacred Elixir*

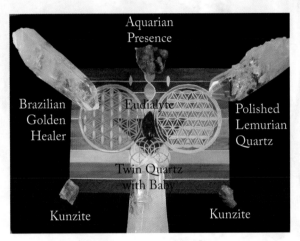

**Resurrection and Balance**
with Signature Crystals

As with Image Key #8, the intensity of
this Image Key is reflected by the intensity
of the background Rainbow Colors supporting the geometry.

The alternating gold and silver filaments
between the bands of color signify the
interweaving of yet another level of
Masculine & Feminine Energies.

The three Quartz crystals are substantial...
weighing five pounds, five pounds and sev-
en pounds respectively. They are all Clear
Quartz, yet have very different energetic
signatures. The Polished Lemurian is very
feminine in nature, the vibrations of the
Brazilian Golden Healer are Masculine and
the Twin with Baby presents a balance of
masculine and feminine energies. Each
of the Signature Crystals contributes
powerful energies to the finished Image
Key.

*Background Colors*

The background colors clearly identify Image Key #8 and Image Key #9 as a pair. They are outstandingly different from all of the other Image Keys.

*Return of the Feminine*
Image Key #8

*Resurrection and Balance*
Image Key #9

We in our Wholeness are Children of the Divine Creator.

We in our Wholeness have perfect Balance between our Masculine and Feminine Energies.

*Resurrection and Balance* is an Image Key to assist us in finding the place of Balance and Wholeness within. This is an Image Key to assist us in remembering that each one of us is a Child of the Divine. We are truly Perfect in our Wholeness.

# ArchAngel Metatron
## speaks* for Resurrection and Balance:

I AM the Holy Grail.

I hold the energies of
the Divine Masculine and Divine Feminine,
coming together in PERFECT BALANCE
to create UNITY in the form of the DIVINE CHILD.

DNA activations are offered
as the helix enters the central magenta chalice,
the gold and silver elixirs mixing to create new LIFE.

My joy is to know that I represent YOU
and your full Awakening within this lifetime.

My job is to assist you to the place where you, too,
can recognize this JOY that I AM.

If this all seems complicated and so unlikely...
I ask you to relax and BE gentle with yourself.
You cannot force this transformation into BEING.

It is more a case of ALLOWING
the intricate interplay of energies to progress within you...
within their perfect timing.

The more you are able to relax into the process,
the easier and more graceful
your experience will BE.

*as channelled by Barbara Evans

# Mary Magdalene
## speaks* for Resurrection and Balance:

Creation
of the Divine Child…

that is YOU…

The Holy Grail… stories… myths… legends…
all connected to the Holy Grail…

The realization of the UNION
of the Divine Masculine and the Divine Feminine
to create the DIVINE CHILD…

Energies in perfect Balance…

UNCONDITIONAL LOVE and COMPASSION…
awakened within.

JOY becomes the guiding principle deep within the HEART
firing the PASSION of CREATION.

As these opportunities present themselves NOW;

the possibilities of

CREATING ABUNDANCE FOR ALL ARE OPENED!

IT IS TIME TO CREATE A NEW WAY.

*as channelled by Barbara Evans

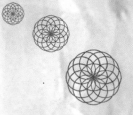

# #10 Wisdom of Solomon

*TEN... We return to #1... New Beginnings...*

TEN... *Wisdom of Solomon* invites our DNA to ignite...
leading us into new levels of Being.

Again the holographic nature of ALL THAT IS comes to
mind... As each individual makes the choice to accept this
challenge of evolution towards being and experiencing full
and true potential, the benefits expand to all of Humanity and
the planet.

AS WITHIN, SO WITHOUT;
AS ABOVE, SO BELOW.

WISDOM is the first guardian of the NEW DREAM.

# Wisdom of Solomon
## Image Key #10

Affirmation #10

I ALLOW the Golden Light of Wisdom to ignite my DNA.

# *Wisdom of Solomon*

## WISDOM...
### First Guardian of the New Dream

Poem #10

Ancient Knowledge sent forth anew.

Messages of golden Light,

DNA activations,

With LOVE and GRATITUDE I receive.

Decree #10

**I AM,**

**I AM,**

**I AM THAT I AM.**

# *Wisdom of Solomon*
## *Image Key #10*

# I AM, I AM, I AM THAT I AM.

*Wisdom of Solomon* and *Transit of Venus* are again paired Image Keys. They were created side by side... both being drawn on the morning of June 6, 2004.

*"Wisdom of Solomon" and "Transit of Venus" Drawings*

June 6, 2004 was the day of an astrological alignment, known as the Venus Transit, during which the planet Venus crossed directly between the Earth and the Sun. This is a rare event which occurs approximately every 125 years. Each Transit is paired. We will experience the second alignment of this pairing on June 8, 2012.

For these two Image Keys, June 6, 2004 was a time in which the wisdom of the Sun (Masculine Aspect) was channeled to Earth through the beauty and grace of Venus (Feminine Aspect).

Throughout the co-creation and unfolding of the Image Keys, I have become increasingly aware of the Guides who support and guide me. Shortly before the Venus Transit, a friend said that she had been told by one of her Spirit Guides that I was about to be told the name of another of my guides.

A few days later, as I took an afternoon "nap" surrounded by crystals, I asked for the name of this guide to be revealed to me... As I awoke the name Solomon was in my mind. I knew immediately that this Solomon was King Solomon referred to in the Bible.

King Solomon is said to have been one of the wisest men to live upon the Earth... His secret knowledge was recorded and hidden within the Temple of Solomon. It is often speculated that these records were discovered by the Templar Knights during the time of the Crusades... and through them, King Solomon's knowledge greatly influenced the development of the Western world. At the time, I was surprised that my guide was King Solomon.

Over the next few days I contemplated the geometry I had been working with for almost a year... the Genesis Pattern...

If the intersecting points of the Genesis Pattern are connected with straight lines instead of circles, two six-pointed stars are created. A six-pointed star with a central point is known as the Seal of Solomon. In this drawing the central point of each star is also the center of the Genesis Pattern.

*Feminine Genesis Pattern*
with Straight Lines of 6-pointed Star

Suddenly, it did make sense that Solomon is indeed a guide for this work…

The timing was so perfect… June 6, 2004 being a perfect opportunity to honor the awareness of Solomon as my guide, and to capture the energies of the *Venus Transit* within Image Key #10, *Wisdom of Solomon*. *Wisdom of Solomon* represents the light of the Sun and its wisdom being transmitted to Earth.

Just weeks earlier my friend, Crystal Jones, had introduced me to a new and special crystal, Indonesian Andara. Indonesian Andara appears to be a volcanic glass formed deep within the Earth. This turquoise colored natural glass immediately captured my heart. The energy of Indonesian Andara is held within the background of *Wisdom of Solomon*. An incredible feeling of love emanates from this crystal, reminding one of the nurturing waters of tropical seas.

Andara is the first Signature Crystal for this Image Key. I connected to three particular pieces of Andara owned by Crystal in order to bring this very beautiful and supportive energy into the Image Keys for the first time.

*Andara Background Colors*

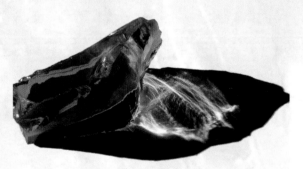

*Indonesian Andara with Crystal Light*

Once the drawings were completed, I needed to prepare for a trip to Colorado. The painting was to be delayed until my return… There was perfection within this delay as I met Star Riparetti of Star Essences during my trip. There was an immediate connection between us as I talked about my work and my desire to use her Orchid Essences in the water for the two images still in process.

Star makes Flower Essences. The ones I was particularly drawn to are made using wild orchids from Maccu Picchu in Peru. The Essences I used come from two series of her Orchid Essences plus one made from the Cantu Flower. I chose five different Essences. Each Essence carries the energetic imprint of a different flower with the name of the Essence describing the gifts embodied within. The Essences used in *Wisdom of Solomon* are called: *Anchoring Light*, *Ancient Wisdom*, *Eternal Youth*, *Gold and Silver/White Chakra* and *13th Gate*.

As the painting was completed, drops of these Essences were put into the water used for mixing the watercolor paints. In addition, I was taking the same combination of Essences as drops under my tongue so that the energy of these orchids and the gifts they carry were infused at every level throughout the process.

*Rose Quartz Heart*

Yet another treasure awaiting me in Denver was a crystal that has been involved in all of my work from this point onwards... a Rose Quartz Heart.

This stone/crystal is about the size of the human heart. The white area is Milky White Quartz. From the top of the heart shaped stone spring beautiful, perfectly formed Rose Quartz crystals.

Acting as the second Signature Crystal for this Image Key, the Rose Quartz heart is very special. The energy vibrations of the Rose Quartz are focused within both the triangle and hexagon at the Heart of *Wisdom of Solomon*.

*Heart of Wisdom of Solomon*

*DNA Helices and Gold Panel*

The central panel above and below the main geometry represents the golden light of wisdom. It is crucial to the energy of this piece.

There are small raised areas within the golden paint symbolizing the information arriving in "packets"... waiting for integration within our Being and within the physical Earth.

Rainbow DNA helices cascading through the Image Key represent the re-connection and ignition of our full complement of cellular DNA.

As you examine the central geometry you will find 12 silver circles are visible... some filled with rainbow light. A 13th circle is hidden beneath the blue, pink and magenta of the center. These 13 circles form what is known as The Fruit of Life.

*Twelve Silver Circles*

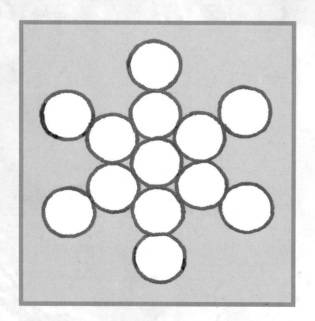

The Fruit of Life is created through the expansion of both the Genesis Pattern and the Flower of Life.

*Fruit of Life*

The importance of this Image Key is certain within my mind. I have come to regard *Wisdom of Solomon* as the FIRST GUARDIAN OF THE NEW DREAM. This links it not only to its paired Image Key #12... *Transit of Venus*... but also to Image Key #11... *Creating the New Dream*.

WISDOM... FIRST GUARDIAN OF THE NEW DREAM...

# ArchAngel Metatron
## speaks* for Wisdom of Solomon:

I AM
the Wisdom of Solomon,
the History of Man.

Golden Light carries the Wisdom of God.

From within this Image Key I transmit this to YOU.

My greatest joy is to assist you in the full activation
of the codes which you carry.

My job is my Joy…

The Golden Light that I carry is infused with the Language of Light
to activate your full compliment of DNA,
awakening those aspects that have been sleeping… for eons of Earth Time.

I assist you to BE a fully realized BEING while still in a physical body.

The greatest Spiritual Teachers to have walked the Earth
have all embodied great WISDOM
and were able to LIVE the experience of LOVE and COMPASSION.

This Image Key is offering to assist you
to place your feet upon this ladder and
begin the active embodiment
of your full and complete
SELF.

*as channelled by Barbara Evans

# Mary Magdalene
## speaks* for for *Wisdom of Solomon*:

Within the Masculine
there is a Feminine principle.

The Masculine downward pointing triangle
represents
Wisdom being brought to Earth.

The upward pointing triangle
represents
the receptive Feminine receiving the Wisdom.

Together they create
both the six-pointed star and the diamond.

The diamond represents
the next stage of Human evolution…

the Ascension to
the Fifth Dimension.

*as channelled by Barbara Evans

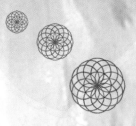

# #11 Creating the New Dream

*ELEVEN... A Master Number...*

ELEVEN... The master numbers are particularly powerful.

It is very appropriate that the first master number falls to *Creating the New Dream*. This Image Key represents the perfect balance of Masculine and Feminine energies.

It represents the energies of the NEW DREAM.

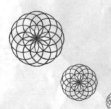

# Creating the New Dream
## Image Key #11

## Affirmation #11

I AM free to Create my highest Dream.

# Creating the New Dream

Poem #11

Perfect Balance within...

All possibilities open...

Integration, a powerful tool...

I am free to choose,

Free to create my highest dream!

Decree #11

**I AM free to Create my highest Dream.**

# Creating the New Dream
## Image Key #11

## I AM free to Create my highest Dream.

What is the New Dream?

The New Dream is based upon...
>    UNITY and PEACE,
>        JOY and BEAUTY,
>            UNCONDITIONAL LOVE and COMPASSION
>                with ABUNDANCE FOR ALL.

The New Dream is founded in True Balance of Masculine and Feminine Energies...
>    Balance within the self...
>        Balance within relationship...
>            Balance within community.

The New Dream brings Awareness of ALL THAT IS...
>    Awareness of being an integral part within the WHOLE OF CREATION...
>        Awareness of being connected to all other Beings and choosing to
>        work together in Group Consciousness ...
>            Awareness of our deep connections to Nature and working
>            together with Nature in Nature Consciousness.

The New Dream requires us to take the best of all that has been accumulated by Humanity: the Wisdom, Knowledge, Love and Compassion... and begin to create anew. The New Dream takes us beyond anything experienced upon this EARTH, beyond even the Golden Ages of the greatest civilizations.

The geometry of *Creating the New Dream* reflects this expansion beyond all other experience.

The drawing of *Creating the New Dream* began on July 30, 2004... a special day of a BLUE MOON... A Blue Moon occurs when there is a second Full Moon within a single calendar month.

As the Crystal grid was formed for the creation of Image Key #11, I was guided to place *Galactic Connection* at the center of the grid directly underneath the center of the table that I use for drawing and painting. *Galactic Connection* is the first Image Key to have the Double Flower of Life… *Creating the New Dream* is the second.

1-Lemurian Jade
2-Fluorite
3-Clear Kunzite
4-Sodalite
5-Hackmanite
6-Smokey Quartz with Garnet
7-Sacred Seven
8-Seraphinite
9-Healers Gold
10-Pink Kunzite
11-Wolframite
12-White Moldavite
13-Chrysocolla
14-Ajoite
15-Lapis Lazuli
16-Rose Quartz

17-Yytrium Fluorite
18-Red Cap Amethyst
19-Quartz struck by Lightning
20-Andara
21-Potential Quartz
22-Champagne Amethyst
23-Rainbow Quartz
24-Aquarian Presence
25-Andara
26-Ajoite
27-Andara

*Center of the Crystal Grid for "Creating the New Dream"*

*"Creating the New Dream"*        *with 24-pointed Star*

The energy of the Crystal Grid radiates from below the table supporting the creation of the new Image Key. Thus the Double Flower of Life within *Galactic Connection* supports and inspires the Double Flower of Life within *Creating the New Dream*.

The star supporting the Double Flower of Life is expanded from the twelve points found within *Galactic Connection* to twenty four points within *Creating the New Dream*.

The knowing came…

The twenty four-pointed star connects us to the awareness of our SOUL and the SOUL of the UNIVERSE. The twenty four-pointed star connects us to our own I AM PRESENCE… the Divinity held within each one of us. The twenty four-pointed star connects us to the source of ALL THAT IS.

The geometry is fully expressed through circles and straight lines. The two are interwoven, supporting each other, offering us a sense of wholeness and completion.

As the gold and silver overlays were being completed, a Mantra developed… This mantra was repeated over and over as my pens spiraled to create the overlay. The sounds of these beautiful words are now interwoven into the fabric of the Image Key itself.

### The Mantra

*Rethreading the Fabric of Society…*
*Rethreading the fabric of our GENES.*

There are four ArchAngels powerfully supporting this Image Key and acting as the Signature Guides: Michael, Ariel, Raphael and Metatron. The central column anchors the energies of the Divine Father, gold, and the Divine Mother, silver, between the heart of the Universe and the Heart of the Earth.

*Star with Gold/Silver Overlays*

The violet is the violet flame of St. Germain protecting these Divine Energies. Beyond the violet flame is the white and gold light of ArchAngel Michael. This expands around the central geometry… which also holds the energy of a Clear Quartz Crystal struck by lightening, providing tremendous energy for transformation.

*Central Column:* Energies of Divine Father, Divine Mother, St. Germain & ArchAngel Michael

The emerald green background carries the blessing of ArchAngel Raphael together with the crystals Malachite, Aquamarine, Ajoite and Emerald.

The Platinum rays radiating through the emerald background carry ArchAngel Metatron's Blessing.

*The Blessings*
of ArchAngels Raphael & Metatron

The rose pink holds the energy of ArchAngel Ariel together with the Rose Quartz Heart used in *Wisdom of Solomon*. The magenta holds the energy of Eudialyte and is blessed by Lady Venus Kumara.

*Rose and Magenta*
of ArchAngel Ariel and Lady Venus Kumara

Another significant area of the Image Key is the central Rainbow Heart infused with the collective energy of the Sisterhood of the Rays and Roses... Many of the Feminine Deities and Female Ascended Masters recognized around the world belong to this magnificent group of Spirit Beings.

*Rainbow Heart Center*

*Twelve-Pointed Stars*

The outer twelve-pointed star carries the energy of Lemurian Jade, a beautiful stone from Peru. Lemurian jade facilitates our connection to the Heart of the Earth and our own higher consciousness, while assisting us to recognize the beauty and abundance that is available to us.

The inner twelve-pointed star holds the energy of Indonesian Andara together with blessings from the Star Dolphins and Star Whales who are actively supporting the evolution of Humanity at this time.

Once again, I was guided to incorporate a selection of Star Essences into the water used for painting and to simultaneously take drops under my tongue so that the energies of these beautiful flowers pervaded all aspects of the work. The names of the six Essences used within *Creating the New Dream* are: *Nature Communion, ONE HEART, Sacred Union, Awakened Thymus, Gold and Silver/White Chakra* and *13th Gate*.

This Image Key, which was drawn and painted after *Transit of Venus*, truly represents for me the culmination of five years work, evolution and growth.

*Creating the New Dream* together with the two guardians, *Wisdom of Solomon* and *Transit of Venus*, mark the end of a major phase. *Creating the New Dream* opens a portal that invites participation in new and expanded life experiences.

Before the Image Keys were numbered it became very clear that *Wisdom of Solomon* and *Transit of Venus* are the GUARDIANS OF THE NEW DREAM. As such, they were to stand on either side of *Creating the New Dream*. The order was shifted to accommodate this. At the time I had not focused on the numbering of the Image Keys… It was only later that I realized the added significance… *Creating the New Dream* became #11… its perfect place… as bearer of the first Master Number.

*Creating the New Dream* is a wonderful Image Key to bring into one's life. From the magnificent ArchAngelic support it offers to the crystals and the geometry, it radiates the vibrations and possibilities of the NEW DREAM.

All who choose to connect with this Image Key are offered an opportunity to bring themselves into resonance with all that it has to offer... the wholeness, fullness, awareness and connection to ALL THAT LIFE CAN BE.

# ArchAngel Metatron
## speaks* for Creating the New Dream:

I AM
the Perfect Balance held deep within the
Divine Spark which is YOU.

I can assist you to find the freedom
to see the possibilities that are available to you.

I can assist you to connect with the DREAM that lies within you
and to realize that as a Child of the Divine Creator
you are FREE TO CREATE YOUR HIGHEST DREAM.

My joy is the LOVE which I carry to YOU.

My job is to activate to yet higher levels…
your MIND, your HEART, your EVERY CELL…
creating new pathways within this lifetime
to reach to the FULLNESS and WHOLENESS which you are.

Messages, Guides and Angels abound in this Image Key.

It represents WHOLENESS.
It represents ALL THAT YOU ARE.
It represents you in your Divine Perfection
and invites you
to make this your experience
NOW.

*as channelled by Barbara Evans

# Mary Magdalene
## speaks* for for Creating the New Dream:

Our Dreams
create
the Divine Plan for Earth...


Dreams that come from the place of UNCONDITIONAL LOVE
within the HEART
and
Hold strong COMPASSION for ALL LIFE.


Choose carefully
as you create your NEW DREAM...

Ask for assistance from
your Guiding Angels and the Ascended Masters
as ...

the NEW DREAM for Earth
is a TRUE CO-CREATION on all levels.


We each have an important role to play.


*as channelled by Barbara Evans

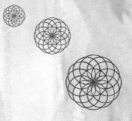

# #12 Transit of Venus

TWELVE...
is the perfect position for *Transit of Venus*.

TWELVE... a sacred number within
many traditions throughout history.

There is mystery attached to the number twelve. In numerology twelve also makes the second three... the 1 + 2 of the 12 = 3... Like a new turn of a spiral, *Transit of Venus* represents a new level of celebration and gratitude. *Transit of Venus* represents LOVE.

LOVE is the second guardian of the NEW DREAM.

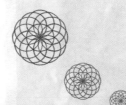

# Transit of Venus
## Image Key #12

## Affirmation #12

# I ALLOW myself to be empowered by LOVE.

# *Transit of Venus*

**LOVE...**
**Second Guardian of the New Dream**

Poem #12

The twelve-pointed star...

A sign of completion...

Layer upon layer healed through LOVE.

Decree #12

**I AM whole... healed through the power of LOVE.**

# Transit of Venus
## Image Key #12

## I AM whole... healed through the power of LOVE.

*Transit of Venus*... the second Guardian of the New Dream... represents LOVE. This Image Key is paired with *Wisdom of Solomon*, representing WISDOM.

These two Image Keys anchor the energies of the Venus Transit that occurred on June 6, 2004, allowing us to continue to work with these wonderfully beneficial energies long after the astrological alignment took place.

*"Wisdom of Solomon" six-pointed Stars*

The geometry of *Transit of Venus* flows from that of its partner.

The six-pointed stars found within *Wisdom of Solomon* are the traditional presentation of such a star... We will call it the Masculine form.

**Feminine Genesis Pattern**
with Straight Lines of Masculine six-pointed Star

This Masculine form of the six-pointed star can be created by joining the intersecting points of the Feminine Genesis pattern. Notice the small inner star becomes rotated to the "Feminine" form.

Here the Genesis Pattern is rotated to its Masculine form and the intersecting points are again joined to create six-pointed stars… The outer star becomes rotated into what we can refer to as its Feminine form, while the small inner star is in the Masculine alignment.

*Masculine Genesis Pattern*
with Straight Lines of Feminine six-pointed Star

If we slide these two Genesis stars together, we find a twelve-pointed star similar to that found within *Transit of Venus*.

*Twelve-Pointed Star*
embedded within the Unity Symbol

The twelve-pointed star is the straight line equivalent of the Unity Symbol.

The magnificence of the particular twelve-pointed star within *Transit of Venus* is that it combines and holds twelve gifts of the Divine Masculine and Divine Feminine…

These twelve gifts are: Grace, Knowledge, Unity, Compassion, Honor, Oneness, Peace, Integrity, Wisdom, Unconditional Love, Gratitude and Joy.

Vibrations of these twelve gifts radiate from the Image Key and invite you to share in their beauty and love.

*The 36 Points of Transit of Venus's*
central Geometry

As your attention is drawn towards the center of the Image Key, you will find that there are three twelve-pointed stars one within the other, contributing a total of thirty-six points in total. The presence of the thirty-six is significant and enhances the flow of energy within the painting.

The innermost twelve-pointed star holds the energy of Lemurian Jade, the middle star carries the energies of Indonesian Andara, and the outer rainbow star is filled with the energies of Red Garnet, Citrine, Aventurine, Blue Lace Agate, Lapis Lazuli and Amethyst.

The Star of Lemurian Jade surrounds a golden hexagon below. Inside the hexagon is found a pentagon filled with rainbow light, holding a five-pointed star. The five-pointed star is a symbol representing Venus...

The center of the five-pointed star forms another pentagon. This time it is silver representing the energies of the Divine Feminine.

The intense magenta background has a pale pink underwash containing the vibrations of Kunzite which flow with liquid LOVE.

The magenta itself holds the energy of Ruby for Life Force, Garnet for Prosperity and Eudialyte for the HEART.

*The Magenta Background*

The Central column has a rainbow helix surrounded by a deep violet/purple. The purple is enfolded by platinum light and beyond the platinum.... pure white light.

I called upon Saint Germain to help with the violet/purple of the central column, asking him to infuse the energy of his Violet Flame of Transmutation into the fabric of the Image Key. This infusion brings Transformational Energy and Freedom into the Image Key to assist with the transmutation of Discord to LOVE and LIGHT... both within the individual and within the environment.

This is important at this time of change as we transform from the Age of Pisces to the Age of Aquarius.

*Violet Flame of Central Column*
with Rainbow Helix, Platinum & White Light

*Horizontal Band*
with Gold & Silver Helix

A horizontal band of Andara energy surrounds and protects the gold and silver helix representing the grids of Christ Consciousness, Grace & Compassion.

This horizonal band together with the central column anchor the energies of the Venus Transit within this physical reality.

*12 Black Discs*
with background of Mary Magdelene

The 12 black discs repeat the pattern found in *Galactic Connection*, Image Key #6, representing expansiveness and movement beyond previous boundaries. The crystal energy within the discs is Lemurian Jade, a stone from Peru.

Lemurian Jade has many gifts to offer... powerfully emanating Unconditional Love and connecting both to our heart and the heart of the Earth. Lemurian Jade provides yet another anchor within the Image Key to support our expansion to realize our Wholeness and true Potential.

The bright magenta between the twelve discs and twelve-pointed star again carries the energies of Eudialyte and is blessed by Mary Magdalene.

Lady Venus Kumara is the most prominent signature guide for *Transit of Venus*... She over-lighted the entire process for this Image Key. Lady Venus Kumara is the Twin Flame of our planetary Logos... Sanat Kumara. They each have powerful connections to the planet Venus and planet Earth.

Once more "Andean Orchid Essences of Machu Picchu" by Star Essences, are incorporated into the fabric of the Image Key. This was accomplished through the seeding of the flower essences into the water used in the watercolor painting. and through me taking drops under my tongue. Essences within *Transit of Venus* are *Divine Goddess, Faith & Courage, High Frequency, Magenta-Zeal Point Chakra* and *13th Gate*.

The inclusion of Star's flower essences within Image Keys #10, #11 & #12 adds new depth and intricacy to the healing vibrations radiating from each one. The essences strengthen the connection to the Plant Kingdom and to the ancient sacred site of Machu Picchu... It is a very exciting and awesome combination. I am most grateful for my connection and friendship with Star Riparetti and the healing knowledge she has shared with me.

All aspects of *Transit of Venus* come together in synergy... in alchemy... to present vibrations of LOVE.

LOVE... SECOND GUARDIAN OF THE NEW DREAM...

*Transit of Venus* is a beautiful Image Key to work with alone.

To work with *Wisdom of Solomn* and *Transit of Venus* as a pair is very supportive in all situations.

*Wisdom of Solomon*

*Transit of Venus*

You may choose to meditate/contemplate the two images or simply display the book at this page to allow their vibrations to emanate into your room.

Working with the full Trio... *Wisdom of Solomn, Creating the New Dream* and *Transit of Venus* is even more powerful. The full Trio anchors the energies of the NEW DREAM together with the GUARDIANS of LOVE and WISDOM into the core of your BEING and into the environment in which they are present.

*Wisdom of Solomon*

*Creating t*

*...w Dream*

*Transit of Venus*

# ArchAngel Metatron
## speaks* for Transit of Venus:

I AM
the Queen of the Skies…
I AM LOVE.

My gift to you is LIQUID LOVE
flowing from my geometry and colors.
I AM the partner of WISDOM.
Together we are the GUARDIANS of your Highest Dream.

My joy is to assist this ascension process on Earth…
ascension to BE the full LOVE and LIGHT
of your Spiritual Self within a physical body…
to assist you to live a life of the Higher Dimensions within the physical world…
to assist you to experience your wholeness.

You, my dears, are my JOY.
My job is to help you all I can, and as much as you will ALLOW…
ASK and I will be there for you.

LOVE is one of the most powerful ENERGIES WITHIN CREATION.
PURE LOVE, UNCONDITIONAL LOVE.
Many are just beginning to explore what UNCONDITIONAL LOVE means…
it is the LOVE that we hold for each one of YOU…

LOVE without judgment…
We love you for who you are…
and we love to help you BE who you choose to BE.
LOVE… JOY… FREEDOM… ABUNDANCE…
What is the Dream within your HEART?
Who do you choose to BE?

*as channelled by Barbara Evans

# Mary Magdalene
## speaks* for for Transit of Venus:

This Image Key is unusual.

It represents LOVE.

It represents VENUS and
Lady Venus Kumara, twin flame of our Planetary Logos…
Sanat Kumara.

One might expect the geometry to be circles…
feminine circles.

Yet here we have the twelve-pointed star
radiating out in circles
to create thirty-six points.

The Feminine Principal
is present and awakening
even in the most unexpected forms and circumstances.

TRUST THAT THIS IS SO.

*as channelled by Barbara Evans

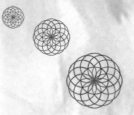

# #13 Cosmic Integration

THIRTEEN... the thirteenth Image Key
represents Christ Consciouness.

THIRTEEN... *Cosmic Integration* holds
the energy of the Divine Feminine
within the pink hibiscus flower
interwoven with the energy of the Divine Masculine
within the turquoise six-pointed star.
Above is the Divine Child...
the Yin Yang Symbol of perfect balance.

Numerologically, Image Key #13 is the second four, 1 + 3 = 4.
Image Key #13 brings the Christ Consciousness level of
Being into our physical world; assisting this higher vibration
to Manifest on Earth.

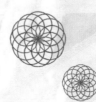

# Cosmic Integration
## Image Key #13

## Affirmation #13

I ALLOW my experience to BE
the KNOWING of ONENESS.

# Cosmic Integration

Poem #13

Feminine and Masculine Interwoven...

There is no Separation.

Connections are made within my Being...

UNITY and LOVE prevail

Awakening the knowing of ONENESS.

All is whole within my BEING;

All is whole within CREATION.

Decree #13

**I AM ONE with ALL THAT IS.**

# Cosmic Integration
## Image Key #13

## I AM ONE with ALL THAT IS.

For a number of years there had been a longing within my heart to visit the islands of Hawaii. A few weeks before beginning *Cosmic Integration*, my dream came into reality.

Many present day spiritual teachers believe that the Hawaiian Islands are remnants of a land occupied by a vast Ancient Civilization known as Lemuria. It is suggested Lemuria existed within the 5th Dimension. Everything was far less physical… much more ethereal than we presently experience within the 3rd Dimensional World. During their Golden Ages Lemurians experienced PEACE, BEAUTY, BALANCE and ABUNDANCE for ALL. It was a period during which the Feminine Energies and skills were strong and honored by society.

As I arrived on Kauai, I could feel my body absorbing the energy of this special land. Recognition of alternate lives awakened within to the extent that there was physical pain within my heart as I energetically recognized the long separation from this place that I loved.

This Pink Hibiscus flower was photographed on Maui. At the time I did not know it would become the focal point of the thirteenth Image Key, *Cosmic Integration*.

Through this photograph I was able to connect with the essence of the Flower as I painted and seeded the energy into the fabric of the Image Key.

*Pink Hibiscus*

Three Views of the five pound
*Polished Lemurian Quartz Crystal*
Playing in the Ocean Waters

One afternoon was spent at an incredible beach... I placed the mighty Polished Lemurian Quartz Crystal, which was first introduced to the Image Keys in *Return of the Feminine*, near the water's edge. The waters of the vast ocean began playing with the crystal... their energies intermingling. This beautiful crystal accepted the gifts, codes and vibrations of the ancient seas... In return the crystal blessed the ocean with the Wisdom and Knowledge held within its crystaline structure. The gifts received upon this day are still held within this crystal and were also transmitted into *Cosmic Integration* during its creation.

*Maui,*
View from the side of the beach

The influence of this Hawaiian adventure is clearly visible within *Cosmic Integration*. However this Image Key was inspired and aligned with a significant astrological event known as Harmonic Concordance II. Harmonic Concordance II occurred on October 28, 2004 and involved five planets forming a QUINTILE, a five-sided Pentagon in the astrological skies.

Harmonic Concordance II followed Harmonic Concordance I of October 2003 when six planets formed a SEXTILE, a six-sided Hexagon.

The geometry within *Cosmic Integration* intertwines the Pentagon and Hexagon.

The Pentagon surrounds the Pink Hibiscus reminding us of a five-pointed star. The energies of the Divine Mother are infused into this flower together with the vibrations of the pink Kunzite crystal shown on page 99.

*Pentagon*
with five petal Hibiscus

The hexagon representing the sextile of Harmonic Concordance I surrounds a six-pointed star infused with the energies of the Divine Father together with the vibrations of Indonesian Andara. This piece of Andara was added to my crystal collection during my trip to the Hawaiian Island of Kauai. It therefore acts as a powerful link to Hawaii, as well as Indonesia.

*Hexagon*
with six-pointed star

Arising from the center of the Hibiscus the stigma, held high, supports the Unity Symbol representing the Divine Child. With both Feminine and Masculine energies in perfect balance, the colors and crystal energies form the Yin Yang Symbol within the geometry... The Divine Child calls us to remember who we are.

There are many different strands to the Divine Masculine and Feminine energies... *Cosmic Integration* takes several of these strands and weaves them together... allowing and encouraging this same interweaving to take place within us as we allow ourselves to receive the gifts of this Image Key.

I regard the energy of both the Divine Father and Divine Mother as being the energies closest to the one source of ALL THAT IS.

*Unity Symbol supported by Style and Stigma*

At the level of Christ Consciousness there are also Divine Masculine and Divine Feminine strands. Masculine Christ Consciousness brings us Unconditional LOVE while the Divine Feminine strand brings us COMPASSION. Both of these strands need to be fully activated and balanced within one's Being in order to reach and experience the level known as Christ Consciousness.

The silver helix found within the gold and silver panels represents the strand of Divine Feminine Christ Consciousness, over-lighted in the Image Key by Isis. The golden helix represents Masculine Christ Consciousness, over-lighted by Serapis Bey. Both Isis and Serapis Bey are deities of Ancient Egypt. The gold and silver paneling itself represents the Masculine and Feminine energies entering our world through major portals within the skies.

*Gold & Silver Paneling plus Helices*

Many Spirit Beings contributed to the co-creation of *Cosmic Integration*...

The Divine Feminine Energy of the Divine Mother was being radiated to all present upon the Earth on the day of Harmonic Concordance II... Both the Divine Mother and ArchAngel Metatron were very prominent throughout the co-creative period of this Image Key.

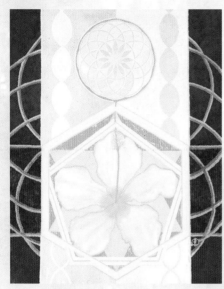

*Expanded Unity Symbol*

As the background was painted, three powerful Spirit Guides were called to participate and add their support... Mighty Poseidon, Greek God of the Sea was called into the deep blue. Pele, Hawaiian Goddess of Transformation was called into the fiery red representing the molten lava of the Earth's core. Gaia, Spirit of our Planet Earth, was called into the nature inspired green.

In order to connect the various parts of the planet on both physical and spiritual levels within the Image Key, an expanded Unity Symbol of gold and silver was placed within the background.

ONENESS

CHRIST CONSCIOUSNESS

These are the energies presented within *Cosmic Integration*.

They are requirements for the full expression and expansion of the NEW DREAM...

These are the ideals that I aspire to... I AM a work in progress!

ONENESS is the absolute knowing/feeling/experiencing of oneself as connected to everything else that exists... including the Source of all creation. Knowing within our heart, we are each a unique aspect of the whole. Everything we do affects everything else that exists... Every unique aspect of the whole is IMPORTANT.

CHRIST CONSCIOUSNESS is the level of consciousness required to enter and viably maintain one's presence in the 5th dimension.

*Cosmic Integration* is the thirteenth and final Image Key presented within this, the first volume of *Messages Of Universal Wisdom*.

As you bathe in the radiating light of *Cosmic Integration* you are invited to… awaken to your full and true potential… to the vastness of your Being… and to the LOVE that you already are.

You are invited to experience the vibrations of ONENESS and CHRIST CONSCIOUSNESS and allow yourself to match those vibrations.

# ArchAngel Metatron
## speaks* for Cosmic Integration:

I AM
the Christed Light in Form.
I bring the energy of the TWELVE together
and represent…
CHRIST CONSCIOUSNESS on EARTH.

My request is that you simply ALLOW yourself
to BE with my energy…
ALLOW yourself to bathe in my
UNCONDITIONAL LOVE, LIGHT and COMPASSION.
ALLOW yourself to absorb and embody the balance
of Masculine and Feminine that I offer.
ALLOW UNITY to BE within you.

My greatest Joy is to embody the Christ Light on Earth
and to BE a BEACON to LIGHT YOUR WAY.
My job is to invite you to grow and evolve to match my vibration and BE…
Experience being a fully realized Christed Being…
a Christal Being …
a Crystal Being…
while still within your physical body upon the EARTH.

This is your opportunity to try this… The energies are supportive…
Your opportunity is to experience
the fullness and wholeness I have placed before you.
It is your choice, a choice we all hope you will accept.
A CHOICE to AWAKEN to
your FULL and TRUE POTENTIAL…
to the VASTNESS of your BEING…
to the LOVE…
THAT YOU ARE.

*as channelled by Barbara Evans

# Mary Magdalene
## speaks* for for Cosmic Integration:

Oh the beauty of this piece!

Bask in its Divine Energies.

There are many facets
to the Divine Masculine and the Divine Feminine…
like facets of a finely cut gemstone.

Here within Cosmic Integration,
some of these facets are placed before you…

interweaving…
layering…
enlightening…
every aspect of your BEING…

…lifting you to your full expression of SELF as an integral part of the ALL.

*as channelled by Barbara Evans

# Epilogue to the Original Thirteen Image Keys

## TWELVE SURROUND THE ONE.

Each of the thirteen Image Keys stands alone as a tool for assisting us to raise our consciousness in manageable steps and to evolve to BE the best that we can BE by reaching our full and true potential as Beings of Spirit within a Physical Body.

The Image Keys are then wonderful and even more interactive and powerful when utilized in a series as presented within this Heart of the Experience.

It is also possible to present them in formation…

1-Indonesian
    Andara
2-Pink Kunzite
3-Potential
    Quartz
4-Rose Quartz
    Heart
5-Fluorite with
    Yytrium
6-Ajoite

7-Citrine
8-Purple
    Fluorite
9-Champagne
    Amethyst
10-Selenite Ball
11-Aquarian
    Presence
12-Red Cap
    Amethyst

*Twelve Surround the ONE*

Twelve Gilcee prints of the thirteen Image Keys surround *Cosmic Integration* within a grid of Twelve Crystals.

The twelve crystals hold the intersecting points of the Genesis Pattern.

*Cosmic Integration* is placed in the center with the other twelve Image Keys between the inner and outer crystals. Imagine each of the twelve Image Keys resting upon the point of a twelve-pointed star.

This arrangement of TWELVE SURROUNDING THE ONE... laid out upon two golden silks overlaid with a third silk of vibrant blues and turquoise color... creates a feeling of COMPLETION and PERFECTION.

A tangible energy of purity fills the room creating a sacred space which is wonderful for meditation and healing.

The Image Keys love to be presented together as a WHOLE... and yes, it is as if each Image Key has its own consciousness... They love to play energetically together creating something far beyond the sum of each of the individual parts.

The journey between September 2003 and October 2004, during which these thirteen Image Keys were co-created, was a phenomenal journey for me... Yet it was also just the beginning of a greater journey. My understanding of the Image Keys is constantly expanding as I continue to evolve and expand, and as new Image Keys continue to be co-created. They are my passion and my life work.

As one who holds this book within your hands, one who reads the words and focuses upon the Image Keys... you are invited to fully ENJOY and PARTICIPATE in this extraordinary journey.

Together we have the opportunity to move ever closer to the full awareness of the VASTNESS OF OUR BEINGS and our place within the ONENESS of ALL THAT IS.

# CHOICE TO AWAKEN

LOVE, BEAUTY, JOY

COMPASSION

FRIENDSHIP, BALANCE, UNITY

# Choice to Awaken

There is a Magic to this process that we call Awakening. It is Magic in the purest sense of the word… It is a Wonder… an opening to the Beauty of our Earth. The Wonder and the Magic is the Choice to live, to see and to experience Love, Beauty, Joy and Friendship.

We can all make this Choice to AWAKEN for it is a Conscious Choice. It is a Choice to release our fears, to jettison the accumulated dross and to live the life of our dreams. It is a Choice that is opening to all who wish to walk this path… a Choice to be made by Free Will as that is the law of our planet.

Many have come into this lifetime upon the Earth to experience Awakening. Many are indeed needed if sufficient numbers are to be gained to reach critical mass… the point at which the Collective Consciousness truly and permanently begins to swing from Fear, Greed and Lack… to Beauty, Joy and Abundance. The shift to the Beauty and Joy of an abundant Universe in which there is more than enough for everyone to have all needs fully and gloriously met is within possibility.

There are no limits to LOVE as LOVE is the power behind all that exists.

When we say, "Yes" and choose to AWAKEN… when we choose Love and Abundance for ALL… we begin a process whereby the right tools and teachers will be presented before us. We open to the natural synchronicities and miracles that exist in everyday life… though sometimes close attention is required in order to notice and fully appreciate these Wonders as they occur.

The Image Keys are one of these tools. They assist us to AWAKEN once we have said, "Yes". They will not and cannot force anyone against their will to evolve… They present an invitation. It is up to each individual, to say, "Yes".

At first this "Yes" may be quietly prompted by your SOUL. It may be a "Yes" that places you in a particular place at a particular time, a "Yes" that peaks your interest and curiosity allowing you to begin the exploration while your conscious mind is full of questions and perhaps uncertainty… for this is something NEW. This "Yes" will take you a certain distance into the spiritual relationship. Then there comes a point where the "Yes" needs to be from a very Conscious place in order for you to deepen your exploration and experience. You will know when this point is reached. It is the point where you truly begin to know from inside of yourself that the Image Keys do make a difference in your life. At this point, you may begin to work with the Affirmations, Poems and Decrees to a deeper and very intentional level OR you may begin to work with the Image Keys in your own very intuitive way…

From this point on, you have set a process in motion and there is no turning back. You have made a Conscious Choice to evolve in this lifetime. This is a Choice to connect with the Being that you truly are, bringing all that you are into this physical world so that you can experience life through your LOVE and MAGNIFICENCE, rather than through Lack and Fear.

This is the most wonderful time to be alive on this planet, as together we birth the NEW GOLDEN AGE. I place this co-creative work before you. It is your choice to proceed.

My intentions are for *Messages Of Universal Wisdom… A Journey of Connection through the Heart* to be a living experience with the Image Keys. The intent is to Support, Inspire and Assist those who choose to AWAKEN.

The expanded intent is to assist the evolution of Humanity both individually and collectively to come to a place of Beauty and Joy, Unconditional Love and Abundance.

This book offers a new beginning in the journey of many who choose to find a New Way of Living and Being within this World… a new way based on the vibrations of LOVE.

The Image Keys are unique to this lifetime. They are an interaction between all that I am, the skills I have accrued in this and other lifetimes, and the Wisdom, Knowledge and Experience of the Spirit Beings who work with and through me. To this is added the New Energies reaching the Earth at this moment in time, which are captured and anchored into the fabric of the Image Keys, together with contributions from the Mineral Kingdom, Animal Kingdom and Plant Kingdom.

The Image Keys are therefore new tools for this time, capturing and anchoring the energies involved NOW, assisting us to integrate them into the core of our Being.

As new tools for this time, the Image Keys encourage us to take the next steps… to use the New Energies combined with ancient Wisdom and Knowledge to move into the next phase of Human Evolution by creating a new age of LOVE and LIGHT… a New Golden Age.

This NEW GOLDEN AGE is something new that has never before existed in the form that we, as a collective, will truly Choose to Create.

We have the opportunity to draw on the best of all of our ancient experience, that we hold as memories within our full 12 stranded DNA. We have the opportunity to use this Wisdom to Create a new paradigm on Earth, a new expression of the full Divine Blueprint for Humanity.

This potential is being supported with these New Energies in ways that are unprecedented on our planet. All is possible NOW.

The plan is magnificent; the opportunities are unlimited.

We are not alone… We are being offered great assistance from many Beings of LOVE and LIGHT who reside within the world of Spirit. There is a Divine Plan for Earth… though many details of this plan are for us, those in physical bodies, to choose and manifest.

Many groups of Spirit Beings have been named as contributors and overseers of this Divine Plan. Here I will name a few of those who have worked with me, though there are many others: the Great White Brotherhood, the Brotherhood of Enoch, the Council of Light, the Inner Plane Ascended Masters, the Sisterhood of the Rays and Roses and the ArchAngels of Love and Light.

This is a Call to AWAKEN.

The Choice to AWAKEN is a Conscious Choice for each individual to make.

This is a Call to AWAKEN to our full and true potential as Co-Creators of our world.

# THE IMAGE KEYS ARE ALL ABOUT LOVE

## CONNECTING THROUGH THE HEART

## TO THE LOVE

## WE ALREADY ARE

# The Image Keys are all about LOVE

L OVE...

Connecting through the Heart to the LOVE we already are,

LOVE in its greatest sense…

All inclusive…
> without judgment…
>> UNCONDITIONAL LOVE.

The LOVE that holds strong whatever we choose to experience in each moment of this life…

> The LOVE that powers the Universe and the Galaxies…

>> The LOVE that silently connects every individual within the web of life…

>>> This LOVE leads us to COMPASSION…

>>> This LOVE is the fabric of our very being.

To learn about and to experience the vibrations of LOVE in the fullest sense while in a physical body is a journey of great depth. It is a journey which many souls presently are choosing to explore.

The Image Keys have been co-created and brought into physical form in response to this desire by so many souls to explore LOVE in its unconditonal form. These are souls who seek to find a new way of living and being within this world.

We are at an important pivotal point in our evolution… This time between 1999 and

2012 will set the foundations for the next thousand years and beyond.

The Choices we make now will powerfully affect future generations.

The Image Keys offer support. They offer a new way of experiencing and connecting, then sustaining the connection to LOVE as a fundamental energy of the Universe.

As we explore, experience and come to know the vibrations of LOVE, we Awaken to a vast web of UNCONDITIONAL LOVE that connects all that exists… We become aware of the ONENESS of which we are a part.

More and more we are hearing how the understandings of the greatest Spiritual Teachers and the theories of the Quantum Physicists are coming together. The same phenomena are being described using slightly different language.

Everything that exists is energy; everything has a vibration.

Pure love, joy and gratitude have high frequencies and vibrations. Anger, fear, hate and disappointment vibrate at far lower frequencies.

Our physical bodies and energy fields record and store all of our experiences, whether dense or light, low or high. The higher vibrations sustain and vitalize us on every level. The lower vibrations tend to build up, leading to blockages in the free flow of our energy fields. If not cleared, these energy blockages contribute to aging and physical disease.

As we come to understand this process, many possibilities open to us. We attract to ourselves what we focus upon.

When we are able to focus upon JOY, GRATITUDE, COMPASSION and ABUNDANCE, we draw these experiences into our lives. If we focus upon fear, failure and lack, then these are the experiences that we draw to ourselves.

The Image Keys are all about LOVE: Love, Joy and Gratitude.

The vibrations of the Image Keys are significantly higher than those of the human body. They are an invitation to raise our vibrations to match theirs. In the process many old, outmoded blockages are brought to the surface for clearing and release. In this way we are able to integrate and carry the higher vibratory frequencies of Unconditional Love, Joy, Gratitude and Abundance in a far more consistent way than previously possible. While this clearing takes place, the Image Keys hold the space... guiding, loving and supporting us.

The Image Keys are therefore not a *quick fix*. The Image Keys are an invitation to enter a journey of Awakening. This is a journey of constantly refining all levels of our being to realize our true and full potential. The Image Keys assist us when our intention is to carry the high and pure vibrations of Unconditional Love, Joy, Gratitude and Abundance within our Being and out into the World wherever we go.

We each carry the full Divine Blueprint within our cells, though much has been deactivated through eons of time. At our SOUL level, many of us are choosing to reactivate the complete Divine Blueprint within our physical expression of SELF. It is this reactivation which will enable us to bring the refined aspects of our true selves into full manifestation. We then manifest the attributes of our TRUE SELF within our physical, emotional, mental and spiritual bodies and fully live them within our daily lives.

The Image Keys assist us to awaken, activate and initiate the Divine Blueprint.

If we wish to enter the New Golden Age, which has been prophesied for so long, these changes are essential. In order to enter the 5th Dimension and create a new way of living and being, it is essential to release and clear the dense energetic baggage that we have carried with us through successive lifetimes.

As we Choose to enter the NEW GOLDEN AGE... we are also choosing to refine all aspects of our Body, Mind and Spirit... choosing to bring our true perfection into our physical form.

When we introduce the Image Keys into our environment, we are saying "Yes" to the high vibrations of Love, Joy, Gratitude, Abundance, Balance and Unity. The Image Keys constantly hold these high vibrations as they assist us to match and maintain them. The Image Keys raise the vibrations of the space in which they are displayed... quietly elevating the vibrations of the room, bringing Peace and Serenity as well as Love and Joy.

As we focus on the Image Keys, we are focusing upon these high vibrational, positive energies, drawing new, positive and joyful experiences into our lives.

The Image Keys bring LOVE and JOY into this world… to assist with the creation of a New Earth and a New Dream for all people. It is a huge vision, yet also a very personal journey.

This is your call to join this vision…

### to Create a New Earth...

### and a New Dream...

### for ALL People.

# DEMYSTIFYING THE MYSTERY

AS ABOVE, SO BELOW

AS WITHIN, SO WITHOUT

I AM CRYSTAL CLEAR

# Demystifying the Mystery

We are, each one of us, vast and unlimited beings, so much greater than our human minds are used to acknowledging and accepting.

All who walk the Earth at this time have chosen to experience in the flesh the Awakening of Humanity and the Ascension of the Earth. We have an opportunity to experience healing, to remember who we truly are while still within the physical body and to create wholeness as we bring the maximum amount of our spiritual selves into this lifetime experience. We are making history within the Cosmos as we strive to move from an experience of duality, of good and bad, of right and wrong, of feminine and masculine, of Love and Fear towards a new experience of Balance and Unity, Unconditional LOVE and Compassion.

So why is it that we are experiencing so much illness, violence and collapse of long established systems? How can this be if we are in such a process of evolution?

Here I present my understanding of where we are and how we might move forward. All is already set in motion, but there are many choices still to make and much work to be done if we are to create the highest version of this New Dream which will form the New Golden Age.

We are the Co-Creators of our World.

Our choices DO make a difference.

For generation upon generation, we have come to experience the physical. We have come to experience the many aspects of what it is like to feel separated from the Source of Creation and All That Is within the Cosmos.

Now we have the opportunity to Choose to remember our Connectedness and our Wholeness. This opportunity has not truly been present until now as the energy has not been at a level high enough to fully support this growth.

The Time of OPPORTUNITY is NOW!!!

In order to achieve this feeling of separation in this experience we call life, our energy has been stepped down enormously from the level of our Soul. We have all agreed to do this before each of our many incarnations.

NOW we have the opportunity to bring more of our Spiritual Self into this life experience... The opportunity is to step our energy back up again.

Many of the experiences we wish to explore in a particular lifetime are planned before incarnating. Thus, as we arrive on Earth, our plan is set in motion. We have already chosen our parents and thus our country of origin and circumstances at birth.

However, there is also FREE WILL. We have many choices to make along the way, and these choices fine tune our lifetime.

From the point of conception we are affected by our genetic makeup, by the genes inherited from our parents.

We also inherit from our parents and direct ancestors the effects of their experiences and culture.

Many of the experiences we inherit are what we would classify as negative, contributing to the fear within the Collective Consciousness. As we each strive to heal these issues within our own lives, we also heal them for our ancestors.

As we grow and develop we accumulate our own experiences of this lifetime and add them to our store of experiences from other lifetimes and of our ancestral line. Some of these are very positive, though many are negative.

We are a storehouse of experience.

In addition to these experiences we are also affected by the stored experiences and history of the land upon which we live. The longer and darker the history of the land, the greater the diminishing effect it has upon our being. In these places, we need to be stronger in order to create a shift.

Where do we store this wealth of experience, both positive and negative? Our experiences are stored within our DNA and within our emotional body. Positive experiences contribute to the love and joy of our lives; negative experiences contribute to the fear and doubt. Our lives become a delicate balance between LOVE and FEAR… the duality of the Earthplane.

If negative fear-based experiences are not released from our emotional body, they continue to build up until they affect our physical systems. Smooth energy flow is essential for good health. When our energy becomes blocked, we begin to manifest disease. As we have become increasingly separated from the awareness of our true nature, we have become increasingly susceptible to a vast variety of diseases.

It has also been my recent experience that injuries in this lifetime often reflect the site of injuries in alternate lifetimes. As we become aware of repeating patterns we have an opportunity to heal on a far deeper level than might previously have been possible.

What is so special about this time on the Earth?

We are at the end of a 26,000 year grand cycle. We are in the time foretold by many throughout ancient history.

We have the opportunity to Choose to AWAKEN to our true vastness as Co-Creators as we enter the Aquarian Age… the New Golden Age.

We have the opportunity to Choose to remember that we are ONE with All That Is. We have the opportunity to remember while still in our physical body that Only LOVE is REAL.

We have the opportunity to remember ONENESS.

We are all connected to each other; we are all connected to all that exists.

What affects one affects the ALL.

We are ALL ONE.

We have the opportunity to create a New Way of Being based upon Balance and Unity.

The driving force behind these changes and opportunities are huge energy shifts. These energy shifts are orchestrated on a vast scale through the movement and alignment of the stars and planets. Bursts of energy are reaching the earth carrying information and codes for our planned Awakening. The effect is intense. Some are more sensitive than others to these energy shifts, but all are affected including the Earth herself. According to Astrologers, the intensity of these energy shifts is set to increase.

As the energy bursts continue to arrive, the vibrational level of the Earth and her inhabitants is being raised. As the level of vibration rises it becomes more difficult to tolerate fear and situations that cause fear. It is as if the old ways are being shaken loose, to rise to the surface, so that they can be dealt with through the new paradigm of love and understanding. This shaking loose applies on both the personal level and the planetary level. Each individual has issues which are rising to the surface bringing awareness and providing the opportunity for healing.

Some will choose to heal; others will not.

For the planet, there are great disturbances in normal weather patterns. Extreme and unpredicted events have been occurring as the Earth herself moves through this process of cleansing and preparing for the new.

As our consciousness rises we develop and refine our understanding of place within the universe and our relationship to all other Beings. It is not easy to define and describe the full picture as that is limited by our present level of consciousness.

Our understanding will grow and expand as we grow and expand in consciousness. However it does seem clear to say… WE are not alone in this experience. Beyond the veil of forgetfulness are many who are waiting to assist us with our process of evolution. I always ask for connection to my Spirit Guides of LOVE and LIGHT, who support me personally. They also work for the highest good, benefiting the evolution of Humanity and the Earth.

These Spirit Guides are willing to guide and assist me with my process, and they are ready to help you as well. The connections I am aware of have developed and progressed as my own vibration has increased. Some of these connections are described within my story.

There is however a Universal Law of Non-Interference. The guides and beings of Love and Light are not able to interfere with our lives of free will. They can only assist us if we ask for their assistance. We have but to ask.

The Image Keys have been a collaborative project. I have been a member of a team that includes spiritual beings, guides, teachers, ArchAngels, many friends and others. I have been assisted and guided every step of the way. The result is that a new tool, the collection of Image Keys, has been provided for these exciting and challenging times.

There is no doubt… Courage is needed in order to follow the inner stirrings of one's HEART.

As the connections to one's guides and inner knowing become stronger, the responsibility becomes greater. Yet Courage is still needed to follow the journey of the HEART.

It is also a journey of JOY and WONDER, of truly feeling alive and grateful for being here.

I invite you to join me on this…

# a Journey of Connection through the HEART.

# JOURNAL ENTRIES

TRUST

TRUST

TRUST

# Journal Entry One

January 2nd 2007

TRUST

SURRENDER

FORGIVENESS

UNCONDITIONAL LOVE

PEACE

BALANCE

UNITY

I TRUST that we will get it right this time.

I SURRENDER to the Divine Plan and Divine Timing,

I FORGIVE myself and others for all transgressions.

I fill and surround myself with UNCONDITIONAL LOVE, transmitting this to all I meet wherever I go…

PEACE comes from remembering ONLY LOVE is REAL.

I maintain my BALANCE and hold the balance for others.

UNITY… We are all ONE.

As this New Year begins, I look at the awareness that has opened up to me. I am so grateful to all those who have assisted me in coming to this place, and I look forward to the next steps.

The beauty, power and love of the Image Keys is beyond all doubt. They are gifts from our Creator to assist the awakening of Humanity and the Ascension of our Planet.

There is a Divine Plan for the Image Keys and their presentation to Humanity.

To this I have said, "Yes".

I have chosen to show up and will continue to do so, as guided.

The plan will unfold in perfect timing with others who have also said "Yes" to the fulfillment of their contracts and have chosen to show up.

The dreams and excitement are building as the time for us to work together arrives, bringing our diverse gifts to work as ONE for the raising of consciousness and evolution… according to Divine Order… evolution to the 5th Dimension and higher.

The feeling is that the time for the Image Keys to "burst" upon the world with LOVE is fast approaching and will make huge strides this year beyond my greatest expectations.

There are as ever many strands and many possibilities.

I ask that all that I do from the simplest task of everyday life to the fulfillment of my Divine Contracts with the Image Keys be done with Beauty, Joy, Grace & Ease from the place within my HEART that overflows with UNCONDITIONAL LOVE.

I ask for protection of all levels of my being from the physical through all levels and dimensions, through to my soul and all of my soul extensions, as I live and love and participate in this we call LIFE…

# Journal Entry Two

## April 17, 2007

I feel the book is beginning to come together. There is an excitement growing inside me. It is wonderful as it flows into being.

I am so grateful to all who are helping and for the experience of this journey I am on.

Thank you to all my guides.

As I read back through eight years of journals I see how far I have come in so many ways. Yet, I also see how clearly I was channeling my Spirit Guides through writing when journaling began in 1999.

It seems that now most of my writing is coming from my Higher Self with the Guides supporting, but not stepping forward except on rare occasions.

Will one of my Guides step forward now to speak to this point?

*Yes, I AM ISIS.*

*You are most accurate in your sensing on both points mentioned. You were already good at this years ago, but did not fully accept or trust your ability. Now you are able to see it clearly as you read your journals. We are delighted to watch you make this connection as you read.*

*Yes, also we are supporting and also standing back.*

*This is a true co-creation on so many levels and you are right. It is so much more than a channeled book or channeled art. You are one of us who is at present in a physical body, equal on so many levels, it is essential that the majority of the writing does come from your Higher Self as this is the way that you are personally going to make the greatest shifts in your own journey to full and true potential... That is what this is all about. Connecting with your Higher Self and bringing all that you are into your physical manifestation of SELF... no small task... but, you are doing very well.*

*Others will recognize the importance of this process as they read the book. It is very different from reading a directly channeled piece from particular members of the 'Spiritual Hierarchy,' as you call us. It is YOU that is forming the fabric of the book. We are in full support and love you dearly as one of us. You truly are a vast and unlimited Being of Love and Light.*

*Continue this intensive work as it is flowing well and is the most perfect timing, as always.*

*You are within a new phase triggered by your recent reading. This will become accelerated as you begin to use the Rose Oil and Rose Essences on a daily basis.*

*Your body has been waiting for this moment for so long. It is hungry for the full essence of ROSE which is so much a part of who you are. It has not had the full nourishment in order to blossom fully until this point.*

*Huge leaps and bounds await you. We watch with great JOY.*

*We love and support you, surround and protect you, even when you forget to ask us. We read your heart constantly. Always you broadcast to us what is in your HEART and we know that your love for all of us is a constant there.*

*You may call on us to contribute when you wish and when it is appropriate. Otherwise we are content to see the connections between you and your Higher Self becoming stronger and stronger by the day.*

*Namaste*

   *ISIS*

ISIS speaks directly to the readers....

*The core of this work is the Image Keys themselves, together with the Affirmations, Poems and Decrees. All other sections contribute to the creation of the essence and flow. Detailed formulas and instructions are not required, as all is held within the coding of the images.*

*This work is presented with gentle grace and quiet strength… Do not be deceived by its simplicity. Its ability to interact and assist with your journey of "ascension" is REAL. It offers a New Way.*

*Namaste*

   *ISIS*

# EXPANSION AND REFINING
# OF THE BODY TEMPLE

## REFINING

## ALL ASPECTS

## OF OUR BEING

# Expansion and Refining of the Body Temple

Expansion and refining of the body temple is an ongoing process which I will share with you through my own personal experience. This does not in any way suggest that others will have the same experience. Each of us has a journey of evolution which is very unique. It depends upon our experiences of this and alternate lifetimes, our life purpose and the ease with which we choose to make the transition from the 3rd dimension to the 5th dimension.

As I look at my own personal journey with the Image Keys, they have made a phenomenal difference. They continually assist me to bring more of my Higher Self into my physical form and have brought more balance, inner peace, joy and wonder into my life.

The process of expansion and refining does, however, require work. I have had to do much inner clearing and cleaning throughout the process of bringing more Love and Light from my spiritual self into my physical form.

As the journey with the Image Keys began in September of 2003, much of this clearing appeared to be emotional in nature. Old emotional wounds would rise to the surface to be released. They were often triggered by an event within my daily life. It has been like peeling off the layers of an onion as the connection was made with ever deeper and deeper wounds… The eventual recognition was that these wounds all represented, in some form, the original separation as my soul began to experience life through the veils of forgetfulness. Simultaneously, the process became easier as there was greater awareness of the process and the reasons for it. This made the release more graceful, at least, most of the time. Whatever triggers challenged the PEACE within; I began to focus on maintaining my inner BALANCE.

During this emotional clearing, I developed a gradual recognition and understanding of my life purpose. This, in turn, powered the passion and self motivation that kept me going through all of the challenges.

A vital piece of the puzzle has been the greater realization and acceptance of who I am, of who we all are, and the place which we hold in the Universe. This realization is that we are setting the energy and foundations for the next Golden Age on Earth. We are responsible for setting the parameters of the new paradigm. We are heralding a new way of living and being within the world. This new paradigm is based on Unconditional LOVE, Peace, Balance, Unity, Compassion and Abundance for all. We have chosen to be here. Each of us has an important job to do as we Awaken and Remember the part we volunteered to play. We agreed with our Higher Self and Guides upon our role in this lifetime before we came into this incarnation.

For me there has also been a physical clearing. Between 1993 and 1999 my health was constantly improving as my spiritual side expanded. Then in April 2001, on my twentieth wedding anniversary, I came down with pneumonia... We were in Jamaica for the perfect celebration. I became extremely sick very quickly. This experience was followed by a second set of illnesses in May 2003. This time it was Lyme Disease and Ehrlichiosis. Again it hit me very suddenly. I experienced bleed through of events of alternate lives that precipitated the pains in varying parts of my body. On both of these occasions I turned to Western medicine for antibiotics to help with the crisis. In both cases a slow recovery followed.

These two events were later described to me as choice points...It was my choice...Was I going to stay and fulfill my mission, or was I going to opt out and leave? Both of the events occurred while my painting was in its embryonic stages. This was before the first Image Key was even a recognized concept. Though I chose to stay on the subconscious level, I was not consciously aware that this choice was taking place. The two events did, however, take their toll on my physical body. As I began co-creating the Image Keys in September of 2003, I was still working with the physical after-effects of Lyme and Ehrlichiosis.

Gradually, I have become physically stronger during the co-creation of the Image Keys.

Then in February 2006, my lower back suddenly went out... The right sacroiliac joint went out of alignment. Over the following months, a series of issues cropped up all on the right side of my body... my right ankle, right shoulder, right knee, right hip and eventually my right thumb. Most could be linked to old injuries within this lifetime. Most also repeated the alternate lifetime experiences that had been previously revealed during the Ehrlichiosis episode. The realization came that often we repeat the same challenges in slightly different form through lifetime after lifetime until we are able to truly heal. I now know we are in a special time where we can heal through all of our lifetimes to regain our wholeness. As we heal ourselves we also heal our ancestors... they truly feel the benefit of the healing we do NOW.

I turned to energy therapists for their expertise, assistance and support, while continuing to use the Image Keys, Crystals, Flower Essences and Essential Oils.

As I searched for answers, attention was brought to the state of my liver and the toxicity stored within the cells of my body. Toxicity had built up over a lifetime of exposure to chemicals and negative emotions, together with the store of negative emotions and experiences from other lifetimes... This led, amongst other things, to a gluten free diet as my body continued working to clear and rejuvenate on these very physical levels.

Even more recently, my attention was drawn to the important influence a major energetic expansion has on the cerebrospinal fluid, the plates of the skull and the sacroiliac joint. If the expansion is unable to flow smoothly into the physical body, one of the most likely symptoms is a sudden misalignment of the sacroiliac joint.

Suddenly, I felt an expansion of my understanding. I had been experiencing expansion crises as my body attempted to adjust to intense rapid changes within.

This understanding helps me enormously as it changes my perspective to one of Refining the BODY TEMPLE.

The refining of all aspects of our Being is TRUE ALCHEMY. It is this process that enables us to move into the 5th dimension and above while maintaining our physicality. As we evolve, the refining of the body temple is essential for the body to carry more love and light, and to carry these higher dimensional energies on a more consistent basis with greater grace and ease.

For me personally, it has been and still is an amazing and exciting journey.

It is also a process that requires commitment and courage. Those who choose to undertake this journey early on ease the way for all who will choose to follow. As we walk this path of awakening to our full and true potential, to the vastness of our being, we contribute to the clearing of the way for all of Humanity. As we connect and fully recognize the Divine Essence that we are, it becomes easier for others to do the same.

We are the Way Showers.

I have fully lived and experienced the Image Keys as they have been co-created. The refining of my body, mind and soul is a work in progress. The Image Keys are a constant presence within my home: in the family room, the entrance hall, my bedroom and studio. They support and sustain these higher vibrations throughout my living and working space. The Image Keys are an amazing gift within my life, filling me with joy. I am forever grateful for their loving presence.

# MAINTENANCE

MAINTAINING A HIGHER VIBRATION

ENFOLDED IN LOVE

VIGILANCE AND ATTENTION

# Maintenance

At this time, in this place of transition, we have to work to maintain a high vibration. It is not sufficient to reach a high vibration and assume we will stay there... Constant vigilance and attention need to be paid to the maintaining and sustaining of this place.

For example, when we visit a spiritual power spot, a sacred place or we attend a wonderful celebration or workshop led by truly spiritual teachers, it is possible to feel the energy and vibration rising throughout our being. We feel inspired, peaceful, balanced, and closer to the ONENESS.

We then return to our daily lives. This is often followed by a gradual fading of those inspiring energies, as if there is a distance placed between them and us. There is, in fact, a movement between the dimensions... We are oscillating between the 5th and 3rd dimensions, depending upon our focus and the energies surrounding us in any moment of time.

As we interact with the 3rd dimensional material world, we are frequently bombarded by lower energies and many lower thought forms... The fear of the collective consciousness and the collective unconscious hangs like a blanket around our planet.

The Image Keys are a wonderful tool for supporting, maintaining and sustaining our higher vibration... They are wonderful for easing our path. The Image Keys raise the vibration of the space in which they are placed inviting all present to sustain or to move to the higher vibratory states. The Image Keys surround and enfold us in their loving energies. They radiate JOY, UNCONDITIONAL LOVE, BALANCE and UNITY assisting with the expansion of COMPASSION.

As we maintain higher vibrations within our own living and working space we create a point of Love and Light upon the Earth.

As the number and strength of these points of Love and Light increase, they are contributing to the evolution of the Planet; they are assisting Gaia with her ascension process. They also contribute to the raising of awareness and consciousness of all Humanity... Each point assists with the thinning of the blanket of fear.

It is through the opening of our HEARTS that we each have the opportunity to contribute to the transformation of the WHOLE, by working with our own energies, our own living space and our place of work. By opening our HEARTS we make it easier for others to do the same. We are creating a path that others may choose to follow... We are working for and contributing to the critical mass required to bring about a shift in consciousness for all... moving us fully into the New Golden Age of Aquarius.

# EQUINOX IN NEW MEXICO

## CELEBRATION

## CO-CREATION

## ANCHORING OF A NEW PARADIGM

# Equinox in New Mexico
## September 2006
### Living, Breathing, Interactive Art Experience

There is a mighty vision for these images called Image Keys… to contribute to the evolution of Humanity and the planet Earth… a New Earth and New Dream for all people.

An important piece of this vision is achieved through this book which you hold within your hands within this moment of NOW. As you read these words, experience the activations and open to the vastness of your True Self, you are contributing to the development of the New Earth.

For this, gratitude and appreciation abound.

Another aspect is brought forth and experienced as the Image Keys travel out into the world to workshops and group ceremonies. On these special trips the Image Keys together with crystals, crystal bowls and the New Earth Connector Template create celebration and ceremony. The New Earth Connector Template is a 12 foot x 12 foot Painted Canvas which forms the foundation on which the Ceremony Grid is built.

The ceremonies bless each place they are invited to BE with the imprint of their energies. A description of one of these events follows… Like looking through a window, you may share my experiences, allowing you to glimpse some of the possibilities. To be within these energies set up for celebration and ceremony is beyond words. My intent is to convey the essence for you to feel as you enter this place…

The Fall Equinox has long been celebrated throughout many different cultures as a time of Balance. The Fall Equinox of 2006, due to the alignment of planetary bodies, was also a time of new beginnings.

The tone was set before leaving New York for New Mexico. The crystals, Image Keys, crystal bowls, New Earth Connector Template and silks to create this living art experience were already packed and shipped ahead in five mighty, black padded boxes.

Four facilitators came together, each bringing unique gifts and energies to the celebration. It became a four day intensive for those who participated with many unexpected, yet delightful aspects... The tone was set, the details yet to take form. We came with open hearts and open minds anticipating a graceful unfolding. We were not disappointed.

A call went out to the Universe with an invitation to participate. We anticipated a response that the room would be filled... and it was. The energy was phenomenal!

On the physical level it was the coming together of myself... a Visionary Healing Artist, Beverly Ausmus Ramsey... in her role as Cherokee Spiritual Elder, Amor Luz Pangilinan... a Gifted Wellness Intuitive and Nina Brown... an amazing Connecter.

As the four facilitators began to unpack the contents of the black boxes, the energies of the crystals, crystal bowls and Image Keys began to intermingle with the sacred ceremonial tools of the Native Americans. This weaving together took place with grace and ease as many points of similarity were already present.

The culmination of the four special days was the creation of a Water Essence. The Water Essence was to hold the imprint of all the energies present. The Image Keys, the crystals, the Cherokee ceremonial pieces, the people and Spirit Guides and a few drops of special water collected by Mayan Grandmother Flordemayo from sacred sites around the world. All came together at the Equinox to capture and anchor the energies of balance and new beginnings.

The intent was for the Water Essence to act as a vehicle through which this synergistic combination of energies could be seeded into the waters of our environment. The purpose of the seeding of the energies is to assist our planet, together with all of Humanity, to move into a state of Balance and Peace.

We dream big!

As everything was put into place, it was possible to feel the energy within the room changing. Anticipation and excitement within the participants was rising. It took most of the morning to prepare and set up. We then went to lunch to allow the energetic pieces to set the energy within the room, so it would be ready for the Creation of the Water Essence upon our return.

After lunch, Beverly our Cherokee Elder, led us on a traditional journey. We each lay down. I covered myself with a blanket of rainbow colored silk. Beverly picked up her ceremonial rain stick and gently began to lead us away from that present moment into a spiritual journey.

She guided us to enter through the gold crystal bowl that formed the centerpiece of our day's arrangement. Below the velvet pillow holding the golden bowl was Image Key #1... *Healing the Waters of the Earth*... and so we moved through this too... moving down into our safe place, our sanctuary.

*The golden bowl is at the center of the New Earth Connector Template*
together with crystals and Image Keys

*Looking into the Golden Crystal Bowl*

Within my meditation, I found myself in a cave of Indonesian Andara.

Andara is a crystal that comes from deep within the Earth and carries a very pure vibration of LOVE... Its appearance reminds me of the warm waters of a tropical ocean, yet it is formed through the action of FIRE. Thus Andara carries the creative, transformative energies of the FIRE ELEMENT in addition to the nurturing, loving energies of the WATER ELEMENT.

*Indonesian Andara on Golden Silk*

## *Meditation*

*The Andara cave seemed fairly small. Walls of Andara surrounded me. The cave closed to a point at the rear, becoming higher as I looked forwards. It was like an isosceles triangle lying on its side.*

Our guide asked us to move towards the altar.

*I moved from my cave into a large open Temple that was also completely built of Andara. In the center of the Temple was a carved altar of this translucent, turquoise colored glass-like crystal.*

Beverly said if we wished, we could place something on the altar...

*I placed the eighteen Image Keys which were completed at this time in a spiral around the altar... They were in their smallest mini-form.*

*We were then guided to look and move towards a path leading away from the altar.*

*I started along the path. We were instructed to look down…*

*I realized that I was no longer walking, but instead was swimming as a mermaid with two star dolphin companions. Their names were Thoth and Serapis Bey and they swam, one on either side of me. Sylvie, a water nymph was also with us.*

*I asked if there was a question to be answered by this journey?*

*"No," I was told, "it is to nourish and rejuvenate you for the next stage of your journey".*

*We continued to swim, and as guided, started to climb. Suddenly we came up to the surface of the ocean. There watching us, was Poseidon, Greek God of the Sea. He did not speak. He just lovingly watched over us as we passed by.*

At this point Beverly stated that we had a choice… We could continue on the path or choose to cross over a bridge that had come into view. The choice was ours.

*I chose to cross the bridge which was completely made of rainbow quartz, sparkling in the sunshine… My companions and I began to cross the bridge. On the far side of the bridge stood White Eagle, in both his human and bird form. He welcomed us into his territory. We stood together for a while, and he presented me with a white eagle feather as a gift. As the two star dolphins, water nymph and I continued, we found ourselves flying looking down on the path below us.*

I heard Beverly's voice once more guiding us back towards the altar…

*As we entered the Temple, it was no longer empty, but filled with many, many Spirit Beings, Archangels, The Inner Plane Ascended Masters, the Sisterhood of the Rays and Roses and more…*

Beverly was calling us to return to our sanctuary, our safe place. I again heard the gentle tinkling of the rain stick calling… calling us back into the room through the painting and the golden bowl… back into our bodies on the Earthplane.

Each one of us had had a wonderful experience and felt replenished… ready for the next step of the day.

# Creation of a Water Essence

A silk scarf lying on the floor formed the entry point to the Crystal Grid laid out within the center of the room, on and around the 12' x 12' canvas called the New Earth Connector Template. As we walked barefoot over this silk, it was as if we entered a different place, a different dimension.

The Image Keys were arranged upon the New Earth Connector Template. The crystals were standing tall and proud on velvet pillows… like powerful universal participants around a council table eager to continue proceedings.

*Creating a Water Essence*

Now it was the turn of the crystal bowls… They, too, told a story. The Divine Mother bowl of platinum and quartz was placed in the South, in the north was the Divine Father bowl of gold and quartz. The Divine Father bowl is light blue, and it also carries plentiful, joyful dolphin energy. The East had the bowl of quartz and ruby for Sacred Union, and the West, a bowl of indium and quartz… which I call the Divine Child.

Spring Water was placed into the four bowls. The four facilitators each played one of the crystal bowls, the tones of the bowls rose and intermingled with the vibrations of the Image Keys and crystals. The sounds and vibrations of each bowl were energetically activating. Gradually, one by one, the bowls were taken to the center and their water was poured into the Golden Chalice. Beverly stepped forward to add the drops of Grandmother Flordemayo's special Water collected from the sacred waters of the world.

From here I led the group on a guided meditation to the Heart of the Earth.

## *Guided Meditation*

*We were greeted by spirit guides and the Divine Mother. We were then taken into a Temple in the Heart of the Earth. Within the meditation, within the Temple at the Heart of the Earth there was an arrangement of crystals and Image Keys which exactly mirrored that in our ceremonial room. Within the meditation we were guided to our places around the New Earth Connector Template.*

*In ever increasing concentric circles around us were those who answered our call to participate.*

*We were guided to draw the energy of LOVE through the crown of our heads… drawing the energy down into our hearts. We were then asked to direct this golden light of LOVE out through our hearts into the Golden Chalice. The Spirit Guides around us all did the same. The air was filled with golden threads of living light connecting each Being within the Temple to the water within the central Chalice.*

The Water Essence was completed. It was unique to this moment… to the people and beings present… to the Equinox… This Water Essence now holds the promise of Balance and New Beginnings together with many, many blessings of Universal Energy.

For the second time that day, we returned from our journey to the room in which we began. The precious water of the Water Essence was poured into bottles, making it ready for distribution. It was now ready for those who would carry it around the globe seeding the healing energies of transformation into the environment, encouraging the development of Balance, Peace and New Beginnings on Earth.

For those who participated… it has been a day to remember forever. It was a living, breathing experience that took us to places beyond the present moment. It has been a day of weaving together the energies of Earth and Sky, bringing the energies of the higher dimensions and weaving them into the physical plane of the Earth. The events of the day were a very real and precious gift. These Gifts are still unfolding within each of our lives and within the planet herself.

It had been a day of beauty and gratitude, a day of shifting and moving beyond boundaries.

There was one additional exciting aspect to this Equinox Celebration. Nina, was preparing to leave on a journey to Northern India. She would attend the Fourth International Council of the Thirteen Indigenous Grandmothers to be convened in Dharamsala, home of the Dalai Lama.

Our work on this day had already been connected to the Grandmothers through the water gifted by Grandmother Flordemayo. To further this connection, prints of the Image Keys from within the sacred layout upon the New Earth Connector Template would be sent to India to be presented to the International Council of Thirteen Indigenous Grandmothers. From India, the Image Keys would travel to each of the Grandmothers' homes throughout the world: to Nepal and the Arctic Circle, to Gabon in Africa and the Amazonian Rainforest of South America, to Mexico and several states within the United States.

As a final stage in the preparation of the prints, the Golden Bowl was played directly above each print. This activated to yet higher levels the codes within each Image Key. We focused with great joy on their destinations and the thirteen Grandmothers who would become their new keepers and guardians.

While Nina was in India, there was a satellite link to the Bioneers Conference in California... A set of the Image Keys was present there, too. Thus we created a geographical grand triangle of energy between India, California and my studio in New York.

On returning to New York, in co-ordination with some major astrological alignments and the Grandmothers' Council, I began working on Image Key #19 called *Children of Light*. The sets of prints in the three locations enhanced the energetic links between us. It formed a web of golden light across the planet, assisting with the anchoring of Peace, Knowledge and Wisdom, Balance and Unity with a focus of a new paradigm for Earth.

It is my full intent that events such as the Equinox Celebration in New Mexico will be repeated around the globe, anchoring these very special energies into many countries on all continents.

Celebrations and Water Essences are created with the intention to assist all who choose to fully connect with the golden, healing light of LOVE, UNITY, BALANCE and ABUNDANCE… supporting those who hold the focus of initiating and maintaining the possibility of a NEW DREAM FOR ALL PEOPLE.

ALL who are guardians of the Image Keys, either through connection with this book or Giclee prints, contribute to this healing network.

The Giclee prints were released first, and as these words are recorded, prints of the Image Keys are already present in many countries of the world: Norway, Sweden, England, Ireland, Wales, France, Italy, Spain, South Africa, Australia, Paraguay, India, Nepal, Japan, Vietnam, Canada and many states within the United States including Hawaii and Alaska… paving the way, anchoring the energy, encouraging and energetically supporting our Evolution.

# HOW DID THIS ALL BEGIN?

PIECES OF THE PUZZLE COLLECTED THROUGH TIME

TRUST

PASSION AND INNER KNOWING OF THE HEART

# How did this all Begin?

## The Questions

When I meet new people and show them the Image Keys, one of the first questions I am asked is, "How did this all begin?"

It is to honor the many who have asked that question that I include this chapter.

There is so much to this story. It is my personal journey of awakening.

The questions…

What do I include?

What is most significant?

What will most clearly help others to notice the patterns which are present in their own lives?

What may I offer to help lovingly guide you to your own destiny?

I continue to grow and evolve, expanding and deepening my conscious understanding of who I AM and what it is that I am bringing into this world for all to share.

I have selected a few of the experiences that have formed the foundation of this awakening process. These chosen experiences focus mainly on the period between the initial trigger and the co-creation of the first Image Key.

Many pieces of my life have come together over a period of fifteen years; this now allows me to recognize the greater thirty five year journey that has brought me to this moment.

Underlying it all is a LOVE for the EARTH.

Some of the experiences have been challenging... others delightfully inspiring... all have contributed to the whole... to my transformation and awakening.

# The First Trigger, First Awakenings and a Quest

The first recognizable trigger was the *death* of my father.

At the time I had *no* spiritual structure within my life.

My father had developed prostate cancer after a lifetime of never being sick. Just a couple of days before he left this life, I was sitting by his side, holding his hand while looking into his eyes. Within his eyes I saw his love for me. I also saw tremendous fear and pain. The following words flowed through my mind...

"It wasn't meant to be like this. There has to be another way."

Nothing prepared me for the devastation I would feel as he left the Earth. Without a spiritual belief system, it seemed to me that he had gone into oblivion. I was devastated.

At the time I had no idea how those few words... "It wasn't meant to be like this. There has to be another way"... would mark the beginning of an amazing journey of awakening. The quest to find another way of living, being and leaving this world without fear and pain had been initiated.

My own health had deteriorated during his illness... Exhaustion set off a variety of immune system dysfunctions and allergies. This physical deterioration continued. I became desperate, not understanding what was happening to me or who could help. Western medicine appeared to have nothing to offer.

# Vacation Dream

A few weeks later my husband, three small children and I traveled to Tuscany for a camping vacation that had been booked since the beginning of the year. The camp site with its spring fed swimming pools, town and weather were idyllic. These two wonderful weeks formed a powerful interlude for relieving some of my emotional and physical pain.

One night, towards the end of the two week stay, I had a dream. The quality of this dream was unlike any I could ever remember.

> *Within the dream I was in a small cottage which I did not recognize. My sister and mother were in another room at the back of the building. There was a knock at the door. When I opened it… it was my father. I was so excited!*
>
> *Impulsively, I wanted him to enter. I wanted to run and call to the others. To both of these impulses, my father said, "No." He simply stated, as he stood in the doorway looking young, healthy and serene, that he had come to let me know he was fine and happy. Yes, I could tell the others later, but for now, he had come to see me… Then he was gone.*

This dream changed my life.

From this point on, I knew beyond all doubt that my father not only still existed, but that he was healthy and happy.

That was the beginning!

# Synchronicities

Synchronistic events began to happen. Within one month I met Viviane Hale who introduced me to Shiatsu, Healing, Aromatherapy and Bach Flower Essences. My life and health slowly began to change. As my health continued to improve each week, a powerful curiosity began to grow. I had a driving desire to learn about these new techniques and new experiences. This was a level of life I had not known existed. I began to buy books, oils and essences as I continued to go for Shiatsu sessions.

Suddenly, at this embryonic stage of awakening, my husband's company asked him to relocate to the United States of America. This brought a huge change in family circumstances to accompany the inner personal evolution already initiated. Moving to live in a new country with three young children is not to be underestimated.

About a year after our relocation, I returned to the United Kingdom to visit family.

I also met with a friend of Viviane Hale. This friend was guided to advise me that I needed to develop my spiritual side. When I asked how... he said there was a book that would assist... I would know when I had found it.

For the next six years I studied healing in many forms through various modalities. New teachers appeared just as I needed them. Healing energy began to flow through my hands in the very first Shiatsu training class that I attended.

One day *A Course in Miracles* entered my life in a miraculous way. It began to fill the spiritual lacuna. The cousin of a dear friend invited me to meet some of her friends... She omitted mentioning that her friends spent each Thursday morning reading, studying and discussing a book... *A Course in Miracles*.

As we arrived at the house, she noticed something at the base of the steps... It was a coin... an English 50 pence piece with its very characteristic seven sides. We were in Lyme, Connecticut!

We entered Harmony House, the home of Mary Mulhausen and Elmira Ingersoll. No one had dropped the coin, and no one had recently been to England. My escort handed me the coin saying it must be for me as I was the only English person present.

The reading that day was very appropriate... just what I needed to hear... I listened... All was so new... already, I was deeply touched.

On the drive home I suddenly remembered that my father had given me a similar coin the year they were first minted. I looked at the old scratched coin I now held in my hand... 1969... it had to be close. On arriving home I searched for the coin I had kept all these years... The date on the shiny new looking coin surface was... 1969. Emotion overwhelmed me; this day had been an amazing gift of a new beginning and a powerful confirmation that I was in the right place at the right time...

I knew I had found "the book".

Mary and Elmira became tremendous role models. They opened their home to many spiritual events in addition to the weekly *A Course in Miracles* group. Their hearts overflowed with joy and their minds were always excited to explore new ways and new ideas... They were grounded in a strong, spiritual sense of Being. During my time with them, each in turn celebrated her 90th birthday... and now Mary is over 100 years old!

For me, *A Course in Miracles* and the experiences that accompanied it, were truly life transforming.

## Next Steps: Energy Healer, Spiritual Joy

Gradually I began to do some energy healing work with a few clients. My "practice" was very small. Most who came were friends or friends of friends. As I look back now I realize how important this phase was in my greater training.

Towards the end of this period, each time I began a session the words… "This is not touching enough people"… would flow unbidden through my mind. Each time I observed the words, but I did not know what to do with them, so I let them go.

By the end of this six year period my life had changed beyond recognition.

As a family we had relocated from a small English village near Canterbury to East Lyme, Connecticut.

Personally, I changed from being a teacher of Biology and Dyslexic students in England to a Shiatsu and Reiki practitioner in the United States.

Spiritually I had moved from a place of *no* spiritual beliefs to a place with a strong, spiritual knowing.

JOY had begun to slowly nudge its way back into my life. It was only at this point that I began to realize how absent Joy had been for such a long time.

## New Test

Still… I was not prepared for the next event… My mother died suddenly, without any warning, of a heart attack… She was eighty years old.

Although my mother was living in Southeastern England and I was in the United States, we talked on the phone several times each week.

This particular week was different. I did not call her and she did not call me… It was as if the Universe had put up a protective barrier between us so that I was not aware of what was going on with her. It was time for her to go and important that I did not attempt to hold her back!

I was about to discover that losing my mother was, and had been, my greatest fear. Although my spiritual self had become strong and I knew my mother was fine, I went into shock. My emotional body shattered.

# Further Healing, New Knowledge

My healing practice stopped. Again I focused upon healing myself. Nine months later I knew deep inside I was still not right. I needed help. I knew I needed to see a medium though I did not know why.

My sister, Jean, had been training with Josephine Gottesville Barber, a very well respected Healer and Medium in England. Jean introduced us. First I had a phone reading, then a few weeks later I went to England for a face to face reading.

A great deal happened within those few intervening weeks.

I reached out to Hillary Filardi who practiced Barbara Brennan Healing Science close to my home in East Lyme. Over the following months, Hillary became a significant mentor on the next phase of my journey.

In one session, just before I left for England, Hillary was wearing a green triangular pendant. I could not take my eyes off this piece of jewelry. My guides suggested that it would be excellent for me to have a similar piece.

I travelled to a store in Rhode Island to buy a pendant for myself and one for my sister. They came with a small card explaining what they were.

I was delighted… Then I wrote in my journal that I needed to find out exactly what I was wearing… I needed to know what a MERKABA was! This was a time before I used the internet. I went to our local Metaphysical store… I asked… "What is a Merkaba?"

The two assistants did not know. At that moment a man entered the store. One assistant said, "He will know…" The assistant presented my question to the newcomer. The man walked straight to a bookshelf and handed me *The Ancient Secrets of the Flower of*

*Life* by Drunvalo Melchizedeck. As soon as I saw the cover of the book I knew I had found something that was to be very important to my life. The cover has a large golden FLOWER OF LIFE on a deep purple background.

This was the first time my eyes were to rest upon this ancient symbol.

There was no time for reading before I began my trip to England. However, I had just read how Edgar Cayce would place a book under his pillow at night instead of reading in the usual sense. Something caused me to do the same with *The Ancient Secrets of the Flower of Life*.

It was a strange night with many pixilated images passing through my mind… all night… though nothing was clear enough for my conscious mind to decipher.

# New Experiences and Learning to Shift

The week that I spent with my sister was phenomenal…

First I attended a Psychic Awareness class with her… I had never experienced anything like this, although I had read of similar happenings.

We began the class by choosing a small Angel Card. Mine was an angel standing with arms outstretched. The angel held in her hands a globe of the Earth together with the word RESPONSIBILITY.

Next a rose quartz heart was passed around the room as a talking stick. Each person was asked to give a message to someone else in the room. Most people present had been attending these sessions for years. They were all very impressive… Two messages were given to me. Both had me in tears as their words connected deeply within my heart.

I felt welcome within this group, yet very inexperienced. I sat waiting my turn, apprehension rising within as I tried to relax and silently asked if there was a message.

All that came into my mind were the earrings I was wearing. I had packed these earrings in my Connecticut home knowing they were to be worn for this occasion. So, I said exactly this… "All that comes into my mind are my earrings".

To me, in that moment, this did not feel like a message.

We stopped for tea. Then, for the first time in many years, our teacher Josephine unexpectedly went into a trance and channeled a Powerful Native American…

Jean immediately began to write the words of the channeling within her notebook.

*Dear brothers and sisters,*

*I bring greetings from friends and family here. It is a great joy to be with you this evening.*

*We know many of you are puzzled by the way we make contact from the spirit world, but we are very pleased with your progress, even if only a few words along the way. These simple words release many kinds of heartache.*

*Many emotions are locked away in your hearts… That is why you have used a Rose Quartz Heart as a talking stick this evening. Every time there are tears, they are tears to clear heartache.*

*Life is not easy on the Earthplane… Being a sensitive is not an easy pathway.*

*As for our dear friend who has traveled across the ocean to be with you… This evening has given her what was in her heart and the earrings…*

*The earrings come from a very great tribe with many great chiefs. She communicates very well with one of those great chiefs. The Great Chief accompanied her and the earrings to bring love and energy to the group.*

*Friend, who made a very great journey to be here, take these earrings now and you will understand that you are far more advanced than you recognize. Sit and develop this way of life. Do you understand?*

The emotions rose within me. Tears overflowed. I cried with love, joy and excitement. So many interwoven emotions were flooding within me.

As we went back to my sister's home that evening, I felt as if I had just experienced the most exciting night of my life. The shift I had made between the first phone reading and this night was huge!

# Personal Reading and Suggestion of Drawing

The personal reading was still to come. As the time approached, I began to feel nervous. I had an inner knowing that somehow this, too, was going to be big!

The reading was tape recorded, and as the tape began, Josephine said, "It is 11 AM on the 11th of the 11th, 1999… Remembrance Day."

Goose bumps went in waves through my entire being.

The reading was beautiful as she connected with my maternal grandparents, together with some of the other guides who are constantly with me. As we both stood to leave the room she added…

"Oh, and try drawing… try drawing faces."

I just looked at her in disbelief and amazement. I had not attended an art class since the age of thirteen. The only drawing I had done was associated with teaching Biology.

As I began my journey home, the suggestion of drawing was uppermost in my mind. The idea of drawing became linked with the strong, unfulfilled desire to walk a Labyrinth on this trip.

I thought to myself, "I wanted to walk a Labyrinth. Josephine said to try drawing faces. I will go home and paint a Labyrinth."

This I did. With the first painting, I knew healing energy was flowing through me into the painting. I knew it was not just for me. It was to be shared with others.

After painting the Labyrinth, I wanted to paint the Flower of Life, but I knew I was not yet ready to do so. Instead I began a short series of paintings, each being a step on my personal healing journey. These included an Egyptian Guide Josephine had described and three Chakra Angels.

*Flower of Life*
on Rainbow Sky

About six months later I was ready to draw and paint my first Sacred Geometry painting called *Flower of Life on Rainbow Sky*. This developed into a series of six paintings, three of which are shown on this page.

*Flower of Life on Rainbow Sky* was the FIRST Flower of Life I drew in this lifetime.

*Colors of Life* was the FIRST painting for which I received powerful guidance within a vivid dream.

*Colors of Life*

*Light and Color*

*Light and Color* is a beautiful Hathor. She was also seen in a dream with the turquoise face adornments forming a five pointed star. She revealed herself as an important guide for these first steps into Sacred Geometry.

For these initial series, I would know that a new painting was coming. Over a period of days, or sometimes weeks, the "knowing" of what it was to be would grow within me... Then I would wake up one day simply knowing that today is the day to paint. The powerful information supplied in dreams were dreams of the same other-worldly quality that is so clear and so memorable. I loved painting! I was so excited with this developing new gift.

Then the paintings stopped! No more ideas, guidance or dreams came! There was no "knowing" that a new painting was to come.

## Crystal Studies

At this point I felt very disappointed that the new gift I was enjoying so much had gone as quickly as it had come. What was I to do next? After considerable time, with contemplation and research, I decided to study Crystal Resonance Therapy with Naisha Ahsian.

As I prepared to start this new avenue of study I was again excited, filled with passion about connecting with the Mineral Kingdom. This course took eighteen months to complete. I loved working with the crystals and with Naisha. Though at times working with the crystals was incredibly challenging; challenging to every aspect of my life through to the core of my being.

The timing of my course increased the initial intensity. My first class was due to begin in mid-September 2001. The world shifting events of 9/11 felt so close to us living in Connecticut. My husband had been working in Manhattan just the day before. Everyone around me knew people who were touched personally through family and friends.

I was due to fly from Boston on September 13 to visit Stonehenge... a trip that was to be delayed for two years. Another trip to be delayed was that of a dear friend due to leave on a pilgrimage to Santiago de Compostella in northern Spain.

As we talked just days after, while still in a state of shock, my friend drew attention to the amazingly high number of Monarch butterflies flying along the Connecticut coast. They seemed to powerfully symbolize the many souls who had suddenly and tragically left their earthly lives.

Within this background, my Crystal Resonance Therapy Training began. One aspect of Crystal Resonance Therapy is the intuitive placement of crystals upon the body of a client in order to bring about balance… balance at all levels of being … physical, emotional, mental and spiritual. It is a "one on one" healing technique. What I had completely forgotten, were the words that passed through my mind as I did the Shiatsu sessions. I was again training to do "one on one" sessions with a client… or so I thought.

During the training with Naisha I did just one small painting… *Wings of a Butterfly*… to represent my Earth Element Crystal Guide, ArchAngel Uriel.

To my surprise, within weeks of completing the Crystal Resonance Therapy Certification, I was painting again.

# More Sychronicities and Problem Solving

It was at this time I completed Reiki Master training in both Usui and Karuna Reiki.

Things began to happen very fast. I showed *Flower of Life on Rainbow Sky* and the other images to a new friend… Suzanne LePick. Suzanne had opened Synchronicity, a metaphysical gift store in our town, the week before we had moved to Pawling, NY. Synchronicity became a source of many incredible crystals and our friendship grew rapidly. Immediately Suzanne recognized the significance of my artwork and encouraged me to get them made into prints.

A couple of months later I exhibited the prints at the first Crystal Conference in Vermont. This event was followed a few months later by an exhibition of the same prints at the Omega Institute in NY, the event which inspired the first Image Key.

During the Crystal Conference an attendee suggested that I needed to build the images so I could get inside. On returning home I pondered this suggestion… How could this be done? The possibility, the desire to do this had been awakened within me… but how could they be built in order to step inside?

I contemplated the three foot diameter Genesa Crystal that graced my garden… The Gardens of Findhorn in Scotland and Perelandra in Virginia, United States, have both chosen to place a copper sculpture of the sacred geometry shape called a Genesa Crystal at their Center. The Genesa Crystal and the Genesis Pattern are different. I have never worked with copper tubing to create sculptures... more contemplation...

My skill is with crystals. I realized I could build the geometry using crystals to form a grid. The crystals within the grid, placed upon the floor, would translate the flat pattern into a complete 3D energetic sphere which I could then step inside. Problem solved!

# Beginning Anew

The paintings already completed were too complex. I needed a simple pattern. I needed a Genesis Pattern to form the basis of my grid.

*The Crystal Wheel*

The *Crystal Wheel* was created specifically as the template upon which to base the FIRST Crystal Grid I was to build and step inside.

Imagine crystals being placed at each of the intersecting points of the geometry. Then the crystals are moved outwards in a direct line from those points, while still maintaining their same relationships. When the grid is large enough, I step inside with my painting table!

The next step was to paint *Crystal Waters*. The creation of *Crystal Waters* was very significant on many levels... It was the first painting to be created within a crystal grid and my first Unity Symbol. A few months later it became one of three original paintings to join me in ceremony at The Chalice Well in Glastonbury. Today it graces the opening page to each chapter of *Messages Of Univesal Wisdom*... like a doorway inviting you to step inside.

*Crystal Waters*

I arrived at the Chalice Well Gardens in Glastonbury, England, with permission to place the three images I had carried from the United States together with some special crystals in a grid formation upon this very special, sacred land.

I began at the "top" by the well itself... moving down through the different gardens, following the path of the water.

*Image Keys and Crystals*
over the sacred spring water

*The Chalice Well*

In the garden, between the Wellhead and the Lion's Head, the Image Keys and Crystals were placed directly over the sacred spring water piped under the lawn.

This is water from a "Red Spring", rich in iron. Over many years it has turned the rocks a bright rust color.

*Image Keys at the Waterfall*

*Paintings and Crystals*
around the Lion's Head
Drinking Fountain

*"Crystal Waters"*
appearing as a blank canvas

At the "bottom" the water flows into the Vesica Pool. The Vesica Pool was the only area I had not placed and photographed the images. It was suggested by the guardian of the gardens that I should do something here, also.

It was a wonderful October day. The sun was shining and the air was very still. I stepped back to take the photograph, then a sudden gust of wind whisked up *Crystal Waters* and dropped it face down in the pool.

*Crystal Waters* is the central image. Taken seconds before the wind gust, *Crystal Waters* appears like a blank canvas, yet it was fully painted.

246 How did this all Begin?

My heart leapt as I dived forward to rescue the painting while hitting my knees hard against the stone. Would the watercolor painting survive? I lifted the wrapped image from the water totally unharmed. I was shocked by this event and contemplated its meaning for a long time.

# Miracle Revealed

It was almost four years later that the underlying miracle was revealed.

I was traveling with the Image Keys through the Los Angeles area facilitating Workshops and Ceremonies with my friend and colleague, Amor Luz Pangilinan. Early one morning I began to relate this particular story. As I did so, Amor Luz connected with what had happened on an energetic level… She described how in those brief moments, three Beings merged with the image bringing their powerful blessings into the piece.

They are the over-lighting Deva of Transformation, Mawu and Isolde. As I have written this story each has stepped forward to present their message to you the reader.

### Overlighting Deva of Transformation...

*You are called to awaken, to make this choice to discover who you truly are.*
*As the Deva of Transformation, I offer you my assistance.*

### Mawu…

*Now is the time to awaken to the beauty and blessings of this world,*
*time to take responsibility for our Mother Earth,*
*for you are the guardians of this sacred place.*

### Isolde…

*Whatever the outward appearance*
*WE ARE ALL ONE.*

There is such beauty in this story with such a strong message. There are often miracles lying just below the surface of our awareness, waiting for us to uncover them, waiting to be discovered as the inspiration that they are. It is an Adventure of Awakening and an Awakening of Adventure. Each journey is its own path.

# Image Keys

I know beyond all doubt that I walk this Earth for a reason. The Image Keys are the reason. I came into this life having made a commitment to bring the Image Keys into the world at this particular time. Their purpose is to assist the evolution of Humanity and the Planet. The Image Keys encourage evolution into the next phase, a higher more harmonious world. This world is in a higher dimension with Unconditional Love, Joy and Compassion.

An integral part of the plan was for me to remain completely asleep until the perfect moment, when Awakening was triggered by my loving father.

The knowing, the expression of this work, comes from many previous lifetimes of experience and connection to: crystals, sacred geometry, healing in many forms, painting and building. As each of the images comes into manifestation, it comes with the sense of me being a builder rather than a mathematician or even an artist. I have come to accept that my intuitive approach to sacred geometry differs from the mathematical way in which many eminent sacred geometers work. Trust has again played an important role here allowing me to develop my own intuitive way.

# Step by Step ... Following my Passions

My journey has truly been revealed one small step at a time. Each step contributes to the development of the whole.

As I followed my latest passion: learning, absorbing, experiencing… then moved on to the next and newest passion, it was not possible to see where it was leading.

To those around me it seemed even more of a mystery.

How could I be passionate about Biology and then Shiatsu and then move on to Crystals? How could painting Sacred Geometry have anything to do with my inner drive to learn about Healing?

My puzzled family observed.

Each and every step was a vital piece of my puzzle from my studies in Ecology, Teaching,

Dyslexia, *A Course in Miracles*, Shiatsu, Reiki, Crystal Resonance Therapy and Sacred Geometry… It all makes sense. Each passion awakened within me connections to alternate lifetimes and the skills, knowledge and wisdom I had previously accrued.

To me now, the pieces of my puzzle are creating a cohesive picture of who I AM and why I AM here.

Now that these many threads have come together I AM ready to share this work. To get my story out, I needed a publisher. It appears that this, too, was part of the Greater Plan.

## My Publisher's Story

Linda McCracken is an integral part of this book coming to fruition. She has also been on a spiritually guided journey. The first inkling for her came in the early 1990s when I was a Biology Teacher and had not heard of the term "Spiritual Awakening".

Linda was given three separate, yet connected messages about her career. With hind sight, these messages bring us to this moment in time. First, she was told by a psychic reader she would be working on a book of sacred geometry and sacred sites. It would have a cover of blue and gold. Secondly, she was told she would be doing incredibly beautiful illustrations in a gorgeous art book. The third message was that she would be working on a beautiful and spiritual book that would be like the Bible, but not.

At the time these readings did not make any sense to her… She began to study sacred geometry and sacred sites, assuming she was to write and illustrate the book, but she did not feel inspired and gradually moved on.

## More Guidance

More recently, a series of steps was orchestrated by her guides. At the time these did not seem related. In 2003 she was guided to obtain a passport. In 2005 she was guided to start a publishing company called "Spiritual Web Communications" that would publish spiritual books. This felt like a natural and inspiring step for her. In 2006 she was guided to go to India to the International Council of Thirteen Indigenous Grandmothers to be held in Daramsala. At least Linda now knew why she needed a passport!

Although aspects of the trip felt really significant… such as when the Thirteen Grandmothers took their group to a private meeting with the Dalai Lama… Linda felt there was another purpose.

Nina Brown, Linda's roommate from India, contacted her upon arriving home. Nina explained that the artist whose Image Keys had been presented to the Grandmothers and to the Dalai Lama, had also written a book. The artist/author was looking for a publisher.

Linda asked to see the manuscript.

When the original manuscript arrived, Linda was excited to notice that in addition to the sacred geometry of the Image Keys, the manuscript also spoke about sacred sites. Then she noticed that the cover design I had included was blue and gold.

Her attention was captured as she realized this was a confirmation of the messages she had received years ago. This was to be the first book published by her company.

# Working Together

As we began to work together, Linda suggested using "fade geometries" to visually assist the explanations of each Image Key. The creation of the fade geometries from the full Image Keys became her artistic participation in the "beautiful illustrations" referred to in the reading she had had years before.

I hesitate to respond to the mention of the Bible… yet one can truthfully say that a number of Beings referred to in *Messages of Universal Wisdom* are also referred to in the Bible.

Linda loves confirmations and continued to be delighted and amazed as members of the Spiritual Hierarchy worked with both of us throughout the editing and layout process… Repeatedly, we received the same messages in different ways on the same day to change, add or delete material… The details received might involve just a single word or the creation of a completely new section. These messages served as important confirmations for Linda and encouraged the blossoming of the manuscript, allowing it to BE the Co-Creation that is within your hands in this moment.

# Summary

*How did this all Begin?* is not my full and complete story... It is a glimpse into the way I have been so powerfully guided through my awakening from "before awareness" to the publishing of this book. At no point did my Spirit Guides sit me down and say... "Here is your 35 year plan"... "10 year plan"... or even.... "1 year plan". I was guided step by step. Everything was done for a reason even though I did not neccessarily see this at the time.

The production of this book has been both a joy and a tremendous growth experience on many levels! Trust and discernment have been constant and vital companions upon this journey. Trust and discernment allowed the co-creation of *Messages of Universal Wisdom* to unfold.

This form of guidance and co-creation is available to all who choose to walk a spiritual path within this very physical experience of Life. Guidance is available to those who ask and choose to be conscious of the LOVE and ONENESS that powers the universe.

We are all connected... we are all part of the ONE.

# TOBY AND THE TEST

## TOBY

## A JOURNEY OF CONNECTION THROUGH THE HEART

## JUNO

# Toby and the Test

Most of this chapter was written during a time I was experiencing raw emotion. For some, reading this chapter may trigger memories of loss of your own loved ones… Know this is good… Allow your heart to release the grief that it is holding… Allow your HEART to HEAL.

I am just a few weeks away from completing *Messages of Universal Wisdom*… NOW I am being faced with a significant heart wrenching TEST. Am I ready and able to walk my talk???

The veterinarians told us our beloved five year old Viszla, a Hungarian Pointer named Toby, has Lymphoma. His prognosis was 4-6 weeks.

Shocked to my core, I drove Toby home. The strength of the bond I have with him is illustrated by the words that flowed through my mind… "How can I go on living without Toby?"

Over the next few days, I gathered all of the tools I had acquired over the last fourteen years and pulled them into operation: Healer friends, Flower Essences, Essential Oils, Crystals and the Image Keys together with Prayers asking for help and intervention from the Spiritual Hierarchy.

The questions came… Why is this happening? Why is this happening NOW? The timing has to be significant.

The very word *Cancer* raises such fear within the collective consciousness of Humanity that you are not only dealing with your own issues, but to a certain extent, everyone else's. As cancer is often associated with the "loss" of a loved one, all past incidences of HEART-felt loss seem to be revisited as the trigger word *Cancer* opens our deepest wounds into raw feelings once more.

My father's experience with cancer triggered my Spiritual Awakening and search for another way of Living, Being and Leaving this world without fear…

WHY at this point, fourteen and a half years after my father left this physical world, am I again faced with a loved one experiencing *Cancer*… At five years old, Toby seems hardly more than a puppy.

The old memories and emotions of the "loss" of my parents are immediately brought into focus.

Has my fourteen year search and quest for another way been for nothing? How have I changed? How is my response different this time? What is my Role? Questions swirl within my mind as I ride this emotional roller coaster.

## WHAT TEST IS BEING PRESENTED TO ME?

I often feel that Toby is an Ascended Master, a Being of a high level of consciousness and great wisdom. It is not for us to choose his path. The glands… lymph nodes… can go back to normal size. He can express his physical perfection within this body.

We love him totally as we know he loves us. So why is this happening NOW, and at this stage in the writing of the book? Am I able to regain and maintain my Balance, Serenity and Love at this time? Balance, Serenity and Love are my Choice.

I ask that my guides assist me on a moment by moment basis to express and experience UNCONDITIONAL LOVE and COMPASSION… to BE in a place of Christ Consciousness while supporting all of my loved ones…

I choose to maintain my Balance through this emotional challenge. I choose to "walk my talk" and stay in a place of Love and Harmony. I choose to continue writing with Toby by my side.

Toby has brought LOVE beyond measure into all of our lives. We thank him.

> *Toby,*
> *You are a truly magnificent and perfect Divine Being.*

As I look at the role Toby has within our family I see how much LOVE he has given and received. I see it is UNCONDITIONAL LOVE. He accepts us exactly how we are and loves us totally.

I feel that we, as humans, are still learning about UNCONDITIONAL LOVE... Toby is our teacher. He has expanded our ability to recognize, experience, give and receive UNCONDITIONAL LOVE.

Beyond this, Toby has been by my side throughout the creation of the Image Keys from #1 - #21. When I paint he is often within the Crystal Grid contributing his energy to the alchemical mix. He is both Guardian and Guide. He brings his masculine form into the grid as I am present in my feminine form, thus creating yet another layer of BALANCE within the Image Keys. He also brings the energy of the Animal Kingdom into the grid in a very powerful way... The more I contemplate his Role in this co-creation... the more I see.

When working on this book, I first write in my journal, then transfer the words to my computer. As I write these words, Toby sleeps on the back of the sofa next to me... his head on my shoulder... his front paw on my chest and his rear paw on my left wrist which holds my journal. It is as if he knows that at last I am writing about his contribution to this work... He is so peaceful in this moment and so am I.

*Toby*

*Toby checking a Crystal's Energy during a Photoshoot*

I know anything is possible... I also know I cannot control the outcome. I cannot heal the cancer just because I want to heal the cancer. So what is my Role?

I inwardly searched to find my BALANCE, to find my Role so that I can understand what I am to do.

I talk all of this through with my sister over the phone... She listens patiently... It becomes CLEAR.

I know I am a channel for Divine Healing energies. I know the energy of LOVE flows through my hands and into Toby. I cannot determine the outcome... That is far beyond my Role.

My Role is to provide him with LOVE each day... to use the tools I have acquired... and to provide LOVE in a peaceful, positive, balanced way with no expectations of the outcome.

Whatever happens will be what TOBY decides he needs to do.

As I have realized my Role, there has been a shift within me and within Toby. It is not my responsibility to determine the outcome. My Role is to hold this place of BALANCE.

The Image Key, *Crystal Visions*, is on top of Toby's crate. The Image Key radiates its love over him as he sleeps at night... I AM CRYSTAL CLEAR... my body, mind and spirit.

Intuitively selected crystals surround him as he sleeps. He happily wears other crystals on a crystal collar emanating their high frequency, healing energies during the day.

I find I have changed during my fourteen and a half year quest to find "another way". This time I have regained my Balance and Inner Peace.

The outcome is beyond my knowing at this moment of writing...

I ask, "Toby... do you wish to speak and to contribute to the book as a whole and to this chapter in this moment?"

As I ask this question, words begin to float across my mind and I know that Toby is communicating with me.

> *Yes, this is my wish.*
>
> *I wish to convey information both to you and to the many readers who also have pets who are important within their lives. It is not just Humanity who is raising its consciousness at this time of great change... So, too, are the many animals, both wild and domestic.*
>
> *Thus the animals, too, are clearing emotional wounds they have collected over "time".*

Pets also have the propensity to take on the woundedness of their human owners. Sometimes when this is very dense and heavy, it settles down into the physical level presenting itself as physical disease. We do this out of choice as a service to the owners we love so much and so unconditionally.

What this present experience is spotlighting is that this process is fluid. All possibilities are open as long as you are able to hold that opening within your mind and consciousness. As owners are able to release their pain, so, too, are we able to release that which we hold for you. It is a fully interactive process. The more aware all involved become, the more we assist each other in the raising of consciousness.

It has been your (Barbara's) belief for some time that I am not an ordinary dog... I ask 'What is an ordinary dog?' We dogs are all great Beings of Spirit who come to Earth to participate in the physical experience. Having said this, I do have to admit that over my many lifetimes, I have collected a vast amount of knowledge and wisdom. I have lovingly brought this knowledge and wisdom to assist Barbara with the creation of the Image Keys. Barbara needed an anchor and that is what I AM. Yet I am not an inert anchor, I AM very active, and channel much energy as Barbara works in painting, writing and healing sessions. In addition, Barbara knows I have helped her clear some great densities carried from other lifetimes, clearings that were essential for the progress of the Paintings to continue.

I love the crystals and the formations Barbara makes with the Image Keys as they connect me with the higher parts of myself and with so many Spirit Beings who support this work. TOBE (Toby) is known and recognized amongst the Spiritual Hierarchy... if this sounds pompous, it is not intended to... I merely wish to expand the vision of many who think dogs are just dogs!

I AM in loving service, I AM honored to be part of this family *and so grateful for the manner in which I have been accepted for who I am and for the opportunities I have received, and for raising my own consciousness while within this physical body. This is a two way street. We have assisted each other to climb to new heights. I AM your constant companion and always will be so… I can work with you from my physical form and I can work with you from my Spirit Being. When you travel I can travel with you in Spirit form even while I maintain my physical presence upon this Earth… Now that you realize that this is a possibility, it will be so… if you would like TOBE by your side as anchor and protector.*

*I LOVE you and each member of the family for who you each are UNCONDITIONALLY.*

I answered…

*My dearest Toby…*

*Thank you for sharing your love and wisdom. I accept your offer of being by my side in spirit form whenever I travel… whichever choice you make about staying in this physical body.*

*I thank you and I am honored by your LOVE and devotion.*

*Barbara*

It is my understanding that in many cases the tendency to develop a particular type of cancer is held within the genetic makeup of an individual, whether the individual be human or animal. There also needs to be an environmental trigger that activates that genetic tendency in order for the particular type of cancer to develop. In Toby's case I have had confirmation from the Spirit Guides that the trigger which initiated the process for Toby was a physical attack by a significantly larger dog which left him with one severe bite and several more minor bites… This attack occurred when his immune system was already being challenged by an Ehrlichiosis infection and the antibiotics being used to counter the Ehrlichiosis.

It was not the physical bites, but rather the density of negative energy associated with this particular attack. The density of the negative energy acted as the trigger for the development of the Lymphoma. Suddenly, I realized I had focused on his physical wounds rather than the energetics.

As time passed, the lymph glands throughout Toby's body continued to enlarge… I continued to question and search for the meaning behind the entire experience… the same questions came up… Why is this happening? What are the lessons?

Finally, I called our Veterinarian to make an appointment. We needed to assist Toby to leave his physical body and move back into the higher dimensions of the Spiritual World.

Throughout the last two days I constantly played Spiritual music, frequently anointing him with Essential Oils such as Lavender, Frankincense and Myrrh. I took some beautiful crystals to the veterinary appointment and laid out a simple crystal grid in the corner of the treatment room to which I added two Image Keys. Then Toby, our Veterinarian and I stepped inside the center of the grid…

It was within my arms, within this sacred space that his Spirit left his body.

Now, just a few days later as I look back on those precious moments, I see how incredibly beautiful they were… He was so peaceful and ready to go.

His spirit left his body on the day of a February New Moon. The New Moon is associated with New Beginnings… I felt this particular New Moon signified Transformation and New Beginnings both for Toby and Myself. It was a powerful energetic day to make this transition… so appropriate for the BEING that he is.

I love him so much… I know he is one of my Soul Mates… I miss the sound of his breath, his touch and his wagging tail… I AM OK… The hole I expected to feel within my HEART seems to be filled… with LOVE!!!

# Addendum One

During the last two days that I spent with Toby I talked to him frequently… I told him that if his Spirit wished to return to our family within a new body we would welcome him with open arms… I know this is possible and know people who have experienced this very thing.

I also asked that if it was not possible for him to return at this time, would he please assist me to find the right puppy... a puppy that would follow in his footsteps... a new Being to contribute to the Image Keys still to be birthed into this physical world, and to be our loving companion.

Within my own mind I imagined this might happen around June, when the weather in New York is warm and good for puppies to play outside. What I did not take into account was that I had clearly stated my request both to Toby and the Universe... As I have heard repeatedly recently, the time between setting a clear intent and it manifesting, is getting shorter and shorter.

To my surprise, following a series of synchronistic phone calls, I found myself travelling on Valentine's Day to meet a new puppy who was just eight weeks old and ready for her new home. She looked straight into my eyes for what seemed like a long time. She then ran and jumped onto my lap as I sat upon the floor.

The week had been intense; the feeling was powerful that Toby was orchestrating this whole event from the Spirit World... I had asked him to help find the new puppy and he set to it straight away...

We welcomed JUNO into our family on Valentine's Day. Before being known as Valentine's Day, February 14 was a day dedicated to the Roman Goddess Juno... I discovered this fact just minutes before leaving home to meet our puppy... We had chosen her name two days earlier!

Juno is wonderful. If Toby was still here in the physical world he would love her... He chose so very well. To Toby I send my continued LOVE and GRATITUDE. You are within my heart forever!

# Addendum Two

It is now six months later. Juno is eight months old and ever more like Toby... both in appearance and some aspects of behavior. Yet she is definitely her own unique being.

When I travelled in California recently, an additional understanding came to me.

I was reading *The Mount Shasta Mission* by Machaelle Small Wright. Machaelle mentions an "X Factor"… something unexpected… something not in the original plan… accidents do sometimes happen.

Suddenly I feel a powerful knowing that the attack on Toby that precipitated the lymphoma was an "X Factor".

What is more… I feel guided to include this new knowing within this chapter. It was the energy held in the land at the point where the attack took place that triggered the other dog to attack. It was this negative energy held in the land that made the energetic density so difficult to shift… so difficult to heal and transmute.

As a result of this density Toby eventually decided he needed to leave his physical body in order to transmute these negative energies.

Toby leaving his physical body at that point in time was not always within his life plan … it was an adaptation to the plan due to an "X Factor". It was a demonstration of his LOVE.

He is now by my side within his spiritual form supporting and assisting me and the work that I do. I LOVE him… I know he is there… I miss his physical presence within my life.

I feel strongly that Juno is connected to Toby in a spiritual sense… she is not Toby returned… it is more like she is a daughter soul… she carries the same purity of Divine Love yet she is far more strong willed, "pushy" and adventurous.

*Juno, "Daughter Soul" of Toby*

# A JOURNEY OF CONNECTION
# THROUGH THE HEART

### TRUST

### PASSION WITHIN THE HEART

### INNER KNOWING

# A Journey of Connection through the Heart

So many people, experiences and events have played a significant role in this journey of discovery... in my Journey of Connection through the Heart. To them all, I am forever grateful. The journey has at times resembled a roller coaster ride as I have searched within myself for the place of Balance. During this time my sense of knowing has grown. My ability to TRUST, slowly expanded.

*Messages Of Universal Wisdom* presents *A Journey of Connection through the Heart* for you to follow as you travel through the energies and vibrations of the Thirteen Image Keys.

The Image Keys offer an opportunity to awaken the connections to your Higher Self, your Inner Knowing, Joy, Wisdom, Love and Compassion. The Image Keys encourage the journey to unfold, allowing the Love and Light that we are to shine through ever more strongly.

Upon this journey, Inner Knowing and Passion are trusty guides... They are valuable connections to our Higher Self.

TRUST in our Inner Knowing and the Passion we feel deep within our Heart allows us to release the need to see the full road ahead.

TRUST allows us to surrender to the flow of each new phase within our life as and when it is revealed.

TRUST allows our timing to be perfect within the greater Divine Plan, even though to our earthly self, there may be a need to develop patience.

Each time I knew I needed to do what I was being guided to do as it felt so right deep within my heart. Gradually as the many threads of my life have come together, I see how each and every step is a vital piece of the personal puzzle creating the cohesive picture of who I AM and why I AM here..

With each choice made, there was an inner fire, a passion, associated with the choice. Years before painting even began, I had a feeling deep inside that there was a job for me to do, although I had no concept of what this was.

As you read my story, I ask...

"What are the passions in your own life which lead you to fulfilling your true and greatest potential?"

Developing TRUST in our own Inner Knowing and Heartfelt Passion allows us to begin.

> TRUST that there is a far greater Divine Plan than any individual is able to imagine.
>
> TRUST that this is a plan we are all plugged into if we choose to pay attention to the inner workings of our HEARTS.
>
> TRUST you can find the role you were meant to play by Listening to the Passion of your HEART!

As we begin to follow our Passion, we start to weave threads of Love and Light upon the Earth which are a blessing to all of Humanity. We are all here for a reason. We are here to connect with our Higher Self and to bring the full Light of our Spiritual Self into this Physical Expression of Life... We are here to discover the Joy and Love which is our esssence.

We truly are Love, Light and Joy. We can bring that essence into every aspect of our daily life. We are here to awaken and experience the Wisdom of our Hearts.

To all who read and experience this
Journey of Connection Through the Heart,
I wish you Love and Joy,
Excitement and Inspiration
and the Courage
to rise to all challenges as you journey
within this Life
to become all that you truly are...

Namaste

# RESOURCES

## MEDITATION

## EXPLORING POSSIBILITIES

## CONNECTIONS

# Meditation
## with *Healing the Waters of the Earth*

*Healing the Waters of the Earth* is the foundation piece for the Image Keys. It is the invitation to participate fully and actively in the transformation to a fully realized Being. *Healing the Waters of the Earth* is the piece that opens the door to allow the process to begin.

You are thanked with gratitude and appreciation for responding to the call heard within your heart, and for saying "Yes" to showing up.

The following meditation is adapted from the form used in an Image Key workshop. Within a workshop, I would guide you step by step through the meditation with my voice. You may wish to ask a friend to read the words to you while you focus upon the Image Key. The words are gentle and flowing…

yet…

It is important to allow pauses for the process to unfold, encouraging the experience to deepen within.

When entering this meditation, you may choose to focus your eyes gently and softly upon the image… keeping your eyes open throughout. You may also choose to close your eyes at any time with the image remaining in front of you.

"NOW you are invited to bring your physical body into a comfortable position in which to journey with *Healing the Waters of the Earth*.

Focus gently upon your breath, inhaling and exhaling gracefully as you draw the life force into your physical form.

*Healing the Waters of the Earth* connects to the Heart, to the waters of your physical body and to your emotional system… The waves of our emotions are like the changing tides upon the shore.

With the next breath, begin to focus on the pink at the center of the image. Pink fills the Unity Symbol bringing Balance and Unity to the Masculine and Feminine aspects within your Being. The pink of Rose Quartz and Kunzite is like liquid love pouring forth from Source.

You are now invited to step inside this glowing pink geometry that stands before you. The pink enfolds you within its pure love, supporting and nourishing you on every level of your Being. The glowing Unity Symbol encourages the absorption of these energies to take place deep within the cells of your physical body. Allow the nourishing colors, crystals and vibrations to touch all aspects of water and emotion held within you.

Turn gently now towards the center of this sphere… See and feel the gold, silver and diamond white light of the lotus petals. These lotus petals radiate pure liquid love and light from Source out in all directions.

As this light touches your heart… your physical heart… your emotional heart… your spiritual heart… very gently begin to respond and draw the vibrations into the very core of your being.

Feel the song of your heart begin to awaken. Take a moment now… listen… do you hear your heart song? It is… the music… the sound and vibration that you are. Be filled with joy as you rest in this place.

Your attention is now drawn outward. The Unity Symbol still surrounds and supports you, holding you gently, cradling you within this place of safety.

Beyond the pink, gold and silver of the Unity Symbol you are further encompassed by the shimmering silver light of an Icosahedron… the geometry of the Platonic Solid of the Water Element.

Through this translucent light, you can see and feel the power and support of the 12-pointed star.

Beyond the star are layers of color… turquoise, amethyst and emerald. Here colors and crystal energies are interwoven to provide nourishment, connection and support for your heart and for all of the water within your body in whichever form that water takes.

As you look up… you see, feel or know… the Rainbow Column of Light is ascending… connecting through the Great Central Sun at the heart of our galaxy right to the Heart of Source.

As you look down… you see, feel or know… beneath your feet the Rainbow Column continues down to the very heart of Gaia. You are so fully and completely supported and connected.

Beyond the turquoise, amethyst and emerald colors, and yet so close, you gradually become aware of a deep vibrant blue. This blue of Azurite and Lapis Lazuli encourages insight and self knowledge.

Within the vibrant blue are many Beings of LOVE and LIGHT who are actively supporting our evolution on Earth… assisting us to reach a place of Love, Peace and Unity.

Take a while to safely and quietly greet some of these beings as they step forward to introduce themselves.

Maybe you see them. Maybe you feel their presence. Maybe it is a knowing that they are present. Maybe a name simply floats across your mind. Know that this is real.

Who is there to greet you this day? Poseidon? Mother Mary? Pythagoras? Coventina? Maybe it is the animals that come forward... the dolphins, the seals, the otters, the turtles... there are many possibilities. Relax and ALLOW the interaction within this place of safety.

You may also wish to listen for the sounds of the waters... the rhythmic ocean waves upon the shore, the thundering sound of a giant waterfall... the gentle patter of rain-drops... the babbling brooks...

Again there are many possibilities... perhaps you see or feel or smell the waters of the Earth.

Know that these beings of love and light are there. They send greetings and blessings for you upon this day connecting you to their higher vibrations.

Enjoy this connection to our guides and mentors, members of the Spiritual Hierarchy who oversee the Healing of the Waters of the Earth.

Enjoy this special connection to our Mother Earth... connection to her physical... emotional... and spiritual body.

Now, consider, is there a specific question within your heart that you wish to ask today?

If so, please pose your question and know that the answer to this question will be given in perfect Divine Timing.

Rest, allow yourself to relax.

Maybe the answer to your question will be received at this time.

Maybe it will come later beyond the time and space of this meditation.

Thank the guides who are present for all that they are.

Thank the guides for stepping forward this day to greet you.

It is now time to return fully to your physical body, to step out of the pink Unity Symbol back into the room in which you started this journey.

Bring with you the memory of your Heartsong if it be in your highest good to do so.

Remain aware of the question you posed together with its answer if that was presented.

The timing will be perfect for each individual.

Begin to feel your body, your fingers and toes. Feel the surface that supports you...

Come back to your physical self and become aware of the physical space where you reside. When you are ready, open your eyes if you have chosen to close them."

Take a few moments in silence to integrate this experience.

Make some notes if you wish.

If appropriate, it may be beneficial for you to go outside... to breathe and move in the fresh air, allowing your feet to touch our Mother Earth. Listen to the sounds of the birds and insects... observe the greens of the plant kingdom, the blue of the sky... Be aware of the natural world that surrounds you... encouraging graceful integration to continue.

Namaste

# Everything Happens for a Reason

Everything happens for a reason...

Every aspect of this book has been co-created with the Spirit Guides. Every aspect of its design has a purpose. The intent is to create flow... flow of energy most easily supported and accessible to all those who choose to enter this experience.

A few examples will be presented so that you may sense the concepts that have been contributing to this overall energy and flow... so that you understand that every aspect of the design has its purpose.

*The Opening begins...*

The most important single symbol within this book is the Unity Symbol. Therefore it is used within the book design to enhance the Balance and Flow.

The two Unity Symbols found on each page of the opening are aligned with the rainbow that is part of *The Crystal Wheel*. These Unity Symbols enhance connection to the HEART of Source and the HEART of the Earth.

Three Unity Symbols guide you into each chapter.

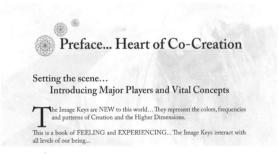

*The Chapters begin...*

*Numerology Page*

A Numerology Page introduces each Image Key... each page has six Unity Symbols... three guide you into the page... three guide you forward to the next two KEY pages.

In the process they create a partial helix through the page reminding you on an inner level of the patterns of your DNA.

As you examine the Image Key Affirmation page, a downward pointing triangle is created by three Unity Symbols... This signifies information from the Higher Realms penetrating through to our dimension.

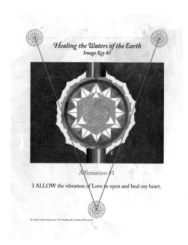

*Image Key Affirmation Page...*

*Image Key Poems and Decrees...*

On the pages with the Poems and Decrees the three Unity Symbols form an upward pointing triangle signifying us striving to Master and integrate the codes, geometries and Language of Light into the core of our Being... Reaching... Allowing... Choosing... Evolution to a higher state of consciousness.

When the pages of the affirmation and poem plus decree are closed together, the two triangles form a third shape... a central diamond... the symbol of the 5th dimension.

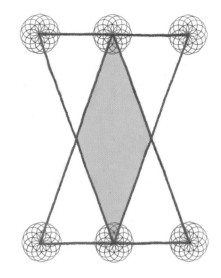

*Diamond with Unity Symbols...*

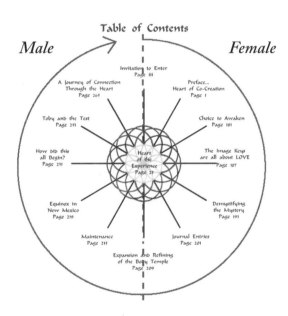

*Resources...*

The Table of Contents Page starts in the 12 o'clock position... moving around clockwise...

This creates a right and left side that represent Male and Female.

*Table of Contents Page...*

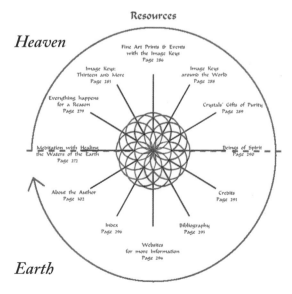

The Resources begin in the 9 o'clock position... moving around clockwise...

This creates an upper and lower section representing Heaven and Earth.

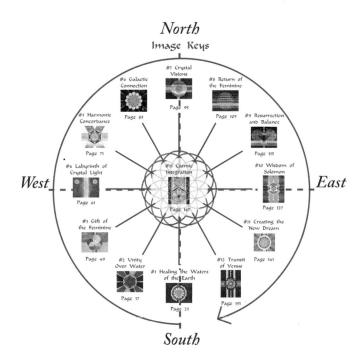

**North**
Image Keys

#7 Crystal Visions
Page 95

#6 Galactic Connection
Page 85

#8 Return of the Feminine
Page 105

#5 Harmonic Concordance
Page 73

#9 Resurrection and Balance
Page 115

#13 Cosmic Integration
Page 167

#4 Labyrinth of Crystal Light
Page 61

**West**

#10 Wisdom of Solomon
Page 127

**East**

#3 Gift of the Feminine
Page 49

#11 Creating the New Dream
Page 141

#2 Unity Over Water
Page 37

#12 Transit of Venus
Page 153

#1 Healing the Waters of the Earth
Page 25

**South**

The Image Key Contents within *Heart of the Experience...* begin in the South... moving around the four directions... South> West> North> East.

These three pages together symbolize the bringing together of Male and Female, Heaven and Earth and the four directions... They represent WHOLENESS.

*Image Key Contents Page...*

The Image Keys are here to empower the individual, to assist you to connect fully with who you truly are in your vastness and magnificence, in your confidence that you are always in the right place to receive the information and wisdom that is for your greatest good in that moment.

As you read, it is likely that certain words or phrases jump out at you and others recede into the background... This is your own inner guidance at work highlighting the parts you need at that time... This is a vital, living, important response for you to notice. These are subtle clues. On another day the words that become *highlighted* may change. Consciously choose to be open as you read. Ask your Higher Self and your Spirit Guides of LOVE and LIGHT to guide you at all times.

*Messages Of Universal Wisdom* is intended to be a book for you to ENJOY... to fill you with PEACE, BALANCE, LOVE and COMPASSION.

As I describe the patterns I see within my life, I invite you to look for your own life patterns... Allow the patterns within this book to help you to see the bigger picture... Allow them to assist you to gain a deeper understanding of your life purpose.

# Image Keys:
## Thirteen and More

The first thirteen Image Keys are a very personal set of Keys for AWAKENING and ACTIVATING the individual SOUL. These thirteen Image Keys are also relevant for group work and can anchor the transformational energies into home and workplace... encouraging all who are enfolded by their energy to raise their consciousness.

*#1 Healing the Waters of the Earth*

*#2 Unity Over Water*

*#3 Gift of the Feminine*

*#4 Labyrinth of Crystal Light*

*#5 Harmonic Concordance*  *#6 Galactic Connection*  *#7 Crystal Visions*

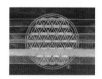

*#8 Return of the Feminine*

*#9 Resurrection and Balance*

*#11 Creating the New Dream*

*#10 Wisdom of Solomon*

*#12 Transit of Venus*

*#13 Cosmic Integration*

# Image Keys #14 - 18

*New Earth Trio*, *Eye of Creation* and *Cosmic Sunrise* have a wider application... They are introducing the energies and vibrations of the 5th Dimension... the dimension that Earth and Humanity are evolving towards in the ascension process.

These Image Keys can also be used as personal tools for transformation, helping to shift the individual into the 5th Dimenison as well as the surrounding space where the Image Keys are located... The Intent of these five Image Keys is to bring the vibrations of Heaven "down" and weave them into the fabric of the Earth on a physical level.

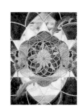

  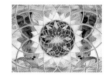

*#15 Shift of the Ages*

*#14 New Earth*      **New Earth Trio**      *#16 Carefree Delight*

*#17 Eye of Creation*      *#18 Cosmic Sunrise*

*Cosmic Column* is the Master Weaver...
alternating spheres of Earth and Sky...
weaving together Heaven and Earth.

*Cosmic Column*      *Cosmic Column*

# Image Keys #19 & 20

*Children of Light* and *Earth Star: Heart of Love* take this a step further. They carry the vibrations of our Full Light Body and Heart Chakra. They contain the codes to support, guide and activate our knowing, our feeling, our AWARENESS, our Divine DNA. They assist us to BE fully awakened... into Christ Consciousness with the full awareness of our Divine Self.

For those who choose to work with *Children of Light* and *Earth Star: Heart of Love*... you are choosing tools to assist yourself to refine and hold the patterns of the higher vibrations while still fully functioning within this world.

*#19 Children of Light*　　　　*#20 Earth Star: Heart of Love*

As we approach 2012, the Language of Light within the Image Keys presents us with new tools and *Messages Of Universal Wisdom* to EASE OUR WAY into the future of our choice as we learn to live in Love and Harmony, Peace and Joy, Beauty and Balance.

Image Keys beyond the first 13 are the focus of future books. New Image Keys will be added to the website as they are created.

# Fine Art Prints & Events
## with the Image Keys

The Image Keys have all been created by hand using a combination of watercolor and acrylic paints plus metallic inks on watercolor paper.

Fine Art Giclee Prints have been made from the original Image Keys through modern technology and the great skills and patience of Lisa and Joe Diebboll at Highland Studio in Cold Spring, NY. The quality of the prints is delightful as they capture the essence, energy and colors of the originals and present them in a form that can be shared by many.

These prints are available on watercolor paper in a variety of sizes from "Mini" to "Large" and on canvas in "Extra Large".

Fine Art Giclee Prints of the Image Keys offer the opportunity to anchor their transformational energies into our homes and workplace in a more permanent way than is possible through the book alone.

The prints invite all who pass before them to match their high vibrations of Love, Peace, Balance, Joy and Abundance.

Many have requested further interaction with the Images Keys in an event setting similar to that described in the Chapter, *Equinox in New Mexico*. The larger Giclee Prints, in GRID formation together with the Crystals of the Grid, become a beautiful, nurturing, activating experience. The sacred energy touches and is felt by the essence of your Soul… by every aspect of your BEING.

In this way the Transformative Energy of the Image Keys can be shared with groups and individuals. This energy initiates, awakens, and supports every level of your Being, EASING THE WAY for the transformational steps necessary to create and experience a NEW EARTH.

Each time the Image Keys and Crystal Grid set out on a journey, it is a very special occasion. Each time the GRID is set up, the Transformational Energy is transmitted to the building and to the land in addition to the people present at the Event. The Sacred Healing Transformational Energies bless the space in which they are set, seeding their very special energetic imprint into the energy matrix of the place.

With the intent of making such experiences possible … Barbara, the Image Keys and Crystal Grid are available for Presentations, Workshops, Activation Experiences and Water Essence Ceremonies.

As with all interactions involving the Image Keys, some individuals will be more sensitive to the energetic interplay and calibrations than others. The energetic shifts will be occurring at the perfect transformational intensity for each person present irrespective of how much detail is being observed by the conscious mind.

If you are interested in purchasing prints or hosting an Interactive Experience with the Image Keys, please check www.crystalwingshealingart.com to contact Barbara. You may also check the website "News" for Event Information!

# Image Keys around the World
## Supporting the Web of Light, Love and Crystal

Our planet Earth has energy bodies in the same way that each human being has energy bodies. Some aspects of these human energy bodies are referred to as auras, chi, meridians and chakras.

Within the Earth the equivalent of meridians are the ley lines or dragon lines. There are also special power points that are similar to our chakras and acupuncture points. Holy, sacred places have been centered upon these power points throughout the world since ancient times.

In addition to the traditional ley lines, there are Light Grids, Love Grids and Crystal Grids within the Earth's energetic system. These grids/energetic pathways have become blocked in many places as a result of the negative actions of many and various human populations throughout history. As with the human body... a smooth flow of energy is required for the Earth to sustain healthy life.

Many Lightworkers are assisting the Earth and her energetic systems to return to a healthy energy flow. They use many different techniques. The Image Keys offer a contribution to the healing process of the energetic systems of our Planet.

Each copy of this book... *Messages Of Universal Wisdom*... and each Giclee print of the Image Keys is a point of Love, Light and Crystal energy within the world. As these books and prints are distributed around the world they continually contribute to the healing process and to the creation of the NEW EARTH. They create a healing grid... They are creating their own Web of Light, Love and Crystal around the Earth.

Some of you may be guided to carry the book and/or prints with you when you journey to Sacred Sites. This process has already been started by myself and others... You are welcome to participate. When the Image Keys visit a sacred site, it enables a mutually beneficial interaction. There is an exchange of energy and codes between the Image Keys and the energy of the sacred place.

Each Image Key contributes to the tranformation necessary to create a NEW EARTH and a NEW DREAM for ALL PEOPLE.

# Crystals' Gifts of Purity

The crystals are vital contributors to the co-creation of the Image Keys in ways that we are not yet fully able to comprehend with our conscious mind. Yet we can feel it in the depths of our Being. Each crystal is an individual contributing to the whole in the same way that we, as humans are each unique, yet at the same time part of the ONENESS.

From the very beginning of my work with crystals, I was interested in collecting crystals from diverse parts of the world. As I began to work with Crystal Grids and channel the energy of the Signature Crystals into the fabric of the Image Keys, I knew, even more strongly, that it was vitally important to bring in these worldwide energies.

A crystal which has been formed in a particular place holds an energetic imprint of that location in addition to the characteristics of the type of crystal or stone. Each individual crystal or stone is truly unique and brings us a gift of its energies.

These crystals, which formed eons ago, hold the Blueprint of the pristine Earth before the many immense traumas of Humanity began to collect and soak energetically into the land. As the crystals are re-awakened and treated with the respect due to a conscious Being, they can assist Humanity to re-connect with the PURITY of the Earth rather than the traumatized Earth.

The crystals that work with and contribute to the Image Keys are carefully selected and awakened. These crystals hold the gifts of Purity together with their "location energies" which are woven into the fabric of the Image Keys. This enhances the ability of the Image Keys to resonate in Harmony with different geographical areas of the planet. In this way the gifts of the crystals are offered to all who choose to work with the Image Keys.

# Beings of Spirit

The Image Keys are a co-creation... I have not worked alone... Many Spirit Beings of LOVE and LIGHT have contributed.

These Spirit Beings represent many races both upon the Earth and beyond. Gods and Goddesses of Ancient Civilizations have come forward together with others including Angels, ArchAngels and Ascended Masters.

These Spirit Beings have great experience and wisdom which they are sharing with us NOW through the vehicle of the Image Keys. They have come together to add their diverse blessings to assist with the evolution of Humanity at this crucial stage of her development.

It does not matter where you come from... where you live... how old you are... who your ancestors are... the color of your skin... your life experience... your social background... THE IMAGE KEYS HAVE BEEN CREATED FOR YOU.

The Image Keys are not a religion; they do not form any part of a religion. Yet they touch the heart of Truth which is present within all religions.

The Image Keys are a co-creative work.

I thank all guides who have contributed and participated so willingly and patiently.

# Credits

Thank you for your contributions to the creation of *Messages Of Universal Wisdom*:

**Lisa and Joe Diebboll**, Highland Studio, NY... for digital capture and preparation of initial digital files of the Image Keys.

**Charlotte Evans**, NY... for the photo of Toby on page 256.

**The Grateful Heart**, RI... for aura photograph of Barbara taken in 2000, shown on page 19.

**Linda McCracken**, B.A., M.L.S., Editor and Publisher, Spiritual Web Communications, LLC, NH... for nuturing and encouraging the development of the raw manuscript into its present form. Linda's inspiration led her to create the fade geometries of the Image Keys which greatly enhance the work. She also took the Andara photo on page 132.

**David Spagnolo**, David Spagnolo Photography, NY... for the portrait of Barbara.

## Book Reviewers... for their beautiful and generous reflections:

**Naisha Ahsian**, Crystal Healer/Teacher. Crystalis Institute for Personal & Planetary Evolution, VT
> *"The keys presented in Messages Of Universal Wisdom are more than simply beautiful images. They are true energetic keys that awaken those who are drawn to participate in their energies. Barbara is truly a channel for timely and important frequencies and knowledge at this critical juncture in the evolution of humanity!"*

**L. Shannon Andersen**, M. Ed., Author. *The Magdalene Awakening*, FL
> *"Through color, sound, light, and the vibration of sacred geometry Barbara Evans invites her readers to experience their own ascension process as they interact with her art, poetry and prose. Through her own spiritual awakening and higher self connection to ALL THAT IS, Barbara demonstrates the universality and availability of angels, guides, and saints; from Mary Magdalene to mythical figures, and she utilizes her higher self to guide readers through her message, her art and the powerful codes available through sacred geometry. Her book is a remarkable tool for opening the heart and shining light on the spiritual path."*

**Carmen Carignan**, R.N.C., Spiritual Healer/Teacher. Tranquil Healing with Angels and Reiki, NH
*"This book is a cornucopia of transformational tools channeled with love and intricate detail. The sacred images within are very moving and multifaceted in use for spiritual expansion. The material in this book is truly astonishing."*

**Marie Dam**, M.D., Integrative Medicine Physician, CT
*"Barbara AWAKENS the world to the New Age dawning. The key images NON-verbally but powerfully accelerate the energies and vibrations of our consciousness towards our Higher Selves and guide us into the New World – the evolution of Humanity. A missing link until now and a beautiful gift to the world. A powerful tool."*

**Dorinda Gay**, Energy Intuitive. Spirit Transitions, NY
*"Messages of Universal Wisdom is a candid personal journey to bring the Universal language of color, symbol and sacred geometry to life. In the heart of the book are the Image Keys, teeming with intricate detail, vibrant color and energy to gently awaken the deepest levels of global consciousness. With her Guides, the author's generous spirit and passion for our planet speak directly to you, the reader, serving as a reminder of the Infinite Love and Divine Wisdom that continually reach out to heal and ascend our beloved Earth."*

**Nancy Hinchey**, Journalist, CT
*"Messages Of Universal Wisdom guides the reader with love and compassion on a journey to awaken and evolve to a new world potential. Through affirmations, poetry and the divinely inspired beauty of the 13 Image Keys, Barbara Evans has created a path to a higher level of awareness. This book is infused with joy, trust and passion, holding to the truth that we can be part of the evolution to a new way of living and being within the world."*

**Diane Hindman**, Ph.D., Publisher, *Natural Nutmeg Magazine*, CT
*"Messages Of Universal Wisdom will touch you in ways you can't begin to imagine. If you have lost a parent, a pet or a loved one, you will truly understand and recognize Barbara's path to awakening as a similar path that you have been on. This book is an exciting journey that we all should experience if we hope to arrive at a global shift in consciousness."*

# Bibliography

Ashian, Naisha. *The Crystal Ally Cards.* East Montpelier, VT: Heaven and Earth Publishing, LLC, 1995.

Andersen, L. Shannon. *The Magdalene Awakening.* St. Augustine, FL: Pelican Press, 2006.

*A Course in Miracles.* Mill Valley, CA: Foundation for Inner Peace, 1999.

Hurtak, James J. *The Book of Knowledge: The Keys of Enoch.* Los Gatos, CA: Academy for Future Science, 1977.

Melchizedek, Drunvalo. *Ancient Secret of the Flower of Life.* 2 Vols. Flagstaff, AZ: Light Technology Publishing, 1998, 2000.

Melody, A. *Love is in the earth.* Wheat Ridge, CO: Earth-Love Pub. House, LTD, 2007.

Raphaell, Katrina. *Crystal Enlightenment.* New York, NY: Aurora Press, 1985.
Raphaell, Katrina. *Crystal Healing.* New York, NY: Aurora Press, 1987.
Raphaell, Katrina. The *Crystalline Transmission.* Santa Fe, NM: Aurora Press, 1990.

Simmons, Robert & Naisha Ahsian. *The Book of Stones: who they are & what they teach.* East Montpelier, VT: Heaven and Earth Pub. , 2007.

Sugrue, Thomas. *There is a River; the story of Edgar Cayce.* New York, NY: H. Holt and Co., [1945].

Twintreess, Marilyn & Tohmas. *Stones Alive!* 3 Vols. Tucson, AZ: TreeHouse Press, 1999; Silver City, NM: AhhhMuse, 2005, 2008.

Virtue, Doreen. *Archangels & Ascended Masters : a guide to working and healing with divinities and deities.* Carlsbad, CA: Hay House, 2003.

Wright, Machaelle Small. *The Mount Shasta Mission.* Warrenton, VA: Perelandra, Ltd., 2005.

# Websites for more Information

Ahsian, Naisha.VT - www.CrystalisInstitute.com
Andersen, L. Shannon. FL - www.TheMagdaleneAwakening.com

Bioneers Conference. CA - www.Bioneers.org

Carignan, Carmen. NH - www.TranquilHealingwithAngelsandReiki.com
Chalice Well. England - www.ChaliceWell.org.uk
Council of the Thirteen Indigenous Grandmothers. India. - www.GrandmothersCouncil.com
Crystal Conference. VT - www.TheCrystalConference.com
Crystal Wings Healing Art. MI – www.CrystalWingsHealingArt.com
Crystalis Institute for Personal & Planetary Evolution. VT - www.CrystalisInstitute.com

Diebboll, Lisa. NY - www.TheHighlandStudio.com

Evans, Barbara. MI - www.CrystalWingsHealingArt.com

Fenn, Celia. South Africa - www.StarchildGlobal.com
Findhorn, Scotland - www.Findhorn.org

Gay, Dorinda. NY - www.SpiritTransitions.com
Grateful Heart. RI - www.GratefulHeart.com

Harmonic Concordance Planets - www.HarmonicConcordance.com/HC-MI.gif
Highland Studio, NY - www.TheHighlandStudio.com
Hindman, Diane, CT - www.NaturalNutmeg.com
Hurtak, J. J., MO - www.KeysofEnoch.org

Jones, Crystal. HI - www.AndaraGems.com

Kenyon, Tom. OR - www.TomKenyon.com

*The Magdalene Awakening*. FL - www.TheMagdaleneAwakening.com
McCracken, Linda. NH - www.SpiritualWeb.org
Melchizedek, Drunvalo. AZ - www.FlowerofLife.org
Mirehiel, Jan & Johnny - www.HarmonicConcordance.com

*Natural Nutmeg Magazine.* CT - www.NaturalNutmeg.com

Omega Institute, NY - www.eOmega.org

Perelandra, VA - www.Perelandra-ltd.com

Riparetti, Star. CA - www.StarFlowerEssences.com

Shell Grotto. United Kingdom - www.shellgrotto.co.uk
Spagnolo, David. NY - www.DavidSpagnolo.com
Spirit Transitions. NY - www.SpiritTransitions.com
Spiritual Web Communications, LLC. NH – www.SpiritualWeb.org
Starchild Global. South Africa – www.StarchildGlobal.com

Tranquil Healing with Angels and Reiki. NH -
        www.TranquilHealingwithAngelsandReiki.com

Wright, Machaelle Small. VA - www.Perelandra-ltd.com

# Index

# About the Author

Barbara's life began in England. After studying at the Universities of Liverpool and Cambridge, she became a teacher of Biology with a passion for the environment.

A spiritual journey of awakening was triggered by the death of her father... Slowly, step by step, the transformations took place including a move to the United States. Six years later, Barbara's dance with Sacred Geometry, Painting and Crystals began. As her journey of awakening deepened, her love and connection to planet EARTH became stronger and far more conscious. She began to feel a powerful desire to visit natural sacred places around the world... Energetic links encouraged by her growing crystal collection.

Within *Messages Of Universal Wisdom* Barbara shares various aspects of her spiritual journey intertwined with the sacred messages of the Image Keys. She strives to inspire others to discover their true passion and potential... to connect with their life purpose and consciously contribute to the creation of a new dream... one that brings a New Earth and New Dream for all people.